# 100 Questions & Answers About Epilepsy

Anuradha Singh, MD
Assistant Professor of Neurology
NYU Comprehensive Epilepsy Center
New York, NY

**JONES AND BARTLETT PUBLISHERS**
*Sudbury, Massachusetts*
BOSTON    TORONTO    LONDON    SINGAPORE

*World Headquarters*
Jones and Bartlett Publishers
40 Tall Pine Drive
Sudbury, MA 01776
978-443-5000
info@jbpub.com
www.jbpub.com

Jones and Bartlett Publishers
Canada
6339 Ormindale Way
Mississauga, Ontario
L5V 1J2
CANADA

Jones and Bartlett Publishers
International
Barb House, Barb Mews
London W6 7PA
UK

Jones and Bartlett's books and products are available through most bookstores and online booksellers. To contact Jones and Bartlett Publishers directly, call 800-832-0034, fax 978-443-8000, or visit our website at www.jbpub.com.

Substantial discounts on bulk quantities of Jones and Bartlett's publications are available to corporations, professional associations, and other qualified organizations. For details and specific discount information, contact the special sales department at Jones and Bartlett via the above contact information or send an email to specialsales@jbpub.com.

**Library of Congress Cataloging-in-Publication Data**
Singh, Anuradha.
    100 questions & answers about epilepsy / Anuradha Singh.
       p. cm.
    Includes index.
    ISBN-13: 978-0-7637-3301-8
    ISBN-10: 0-7637-3301-6
    1. Epilepsy—Popular works.    I. Title: One hundred questions & answers about epilepsy.    II. Title.
    RC372.S574 2006
    616.85'3—dc22

                                                            2005037207

6048

**Production Credits**
Executive Publisher: Christopher Davis
Associate Editor: Kathy Richardson
Production Director: Amy Rose
Production Editor: Renée Sekerak
Associate Marketing Manager: Laura Kavigian
Manufacturing and Inventory Coordinator: Amy Bacus
Cover Design: Kate Ternullo
Composition: Auburn Associates, Inc.
Printing and Binding: Malloy, Inc.
Cover Printing: Malloy, Inc.

Printed in the United States of America
10 09 08 07 06    10 9 8 7 6 5 4 3 2

# Contents

This book by Dr. Anuradha Singh provides straightforward and simple answers to the most common and the most important questions that confront individuals with epilepsy and their families. Dr. Singh avoids the terms that often prove confusing and/or unnecessarily stigmatize individuals. Most importantly, the information communicated in this book will be an important source of empowerment and knowledge for the lay epilepsy community.

The organization of this book provides a road map to navigate through the different potential stages of epilepsy: from the initial diagnosis and questions of whether it is epilepsy, to the adjustment of how to learn to live with the diagnosis and the therapy. The various treatments for epilepsy, mostly medication but also surgery, are carefully explained with consideration to both beneficial and harmful effects.

The book also has specific sections on different special populations. For example, epilepsy in children, where more than 70% of new onset epilepsy cases occurred, is covered in detail. Women with epilepsy confront issues of contraception, pregnancy, potential teratogenic effects of antiepileptic medications, and other issues that are also reviewed.

Dr. Singh also answers your questions about driving and other issues that so significantly impact the quality of life for people with epilepsy. All of this information—from the basic diagnostic studies that doctors do to decide whether a patient does or does not have epilepsy, to the various antiepileptic medications and their side effects, as well as the evaluation and decision issues surrounding the question of epilepsy surgery—is provided.

I highly recommend this book to patients and families touched by epilepsy for the insights and knowledge it provides.

Orrin Devinsky, MD
Director, NYU Epilepsy Center
Professor of Neurology, Neurosurgery, and Psychiatry
NYU School of Medicine

*100 Questions & Answers about Epilepsy* uses a unique approach to give information to patients and their families covering myriad topics. My interaction with patients has taught me that patients need to be more informed about their medical illnesses. My patients taught me to look beyond worrying about their seizure frequency and giving them prescription refills. A few instances had touched my heart during my interactions with my patients; I would like to share some of those with the readers. During my clinical neurophysiology training at New York Comprehensive Epilepsy Center, I was going through the seizure video files of a toddler. I was astonished to watch a mother on the video who would wake up every few minutes in the middle of the night. Her child was having very frequent infantile spasms. Some of the seizures on the video were so subtle that they weren't recognized by physicians, but the mother did not miss a single seizure. This made me realize the impact of this disease on a parent whose child is suffering from epilepsy. Another incident that crosses my mind is when one female patient kissed my hand as I informed her that she could plan a family. She lived with the notion that it was not okay to conceive because she had epilepsy. Once I saw two new patients on the same day. As I tried to put their history together, I realized that two of my very young female patients had recently experienced their first seizure under very different circumstances. One had a seizure while waiting in a subway. During the seizure, she fell on the tracks and lost her left leg. The other patient had her first seizure while she waited at a New Jersey turnpike toll booth. She was safe but kept asking what if she had had a seizure five minutes earlier while she was driving at 70 miles per hour on the turnpike.

*What is epilepsy?* Why do people attach social stigma to this chronic medical condition? In the initial section of the book, I have tried to give basic information of this poorly understood condition.

Different sections of the book address medical treatment options, diagnostic tests, and adverse and beneficial effects of antiepileptics. Women with epilepsy face many controversial issues concerning their reproductive health. Information concerning sexual dysfunction, fertility, effects of antiepileptics on pregnancy and the fetus is often unavailable. Surgical options are touched upon in a simplified manner as another option in medical refractory cases. This book also makes an attempt to cover special issues relating to the extremes of age, namely pediatric and geriatric population. Other topics include non-epileptic seizures, psychiatric comorbidity, and the need to recognize and manage depression, anxiety, and other psychiatric disorders. It is my hope that we develop more effective treatments for epilepsy in the future.

I also want to thank Jared Caponi for sharing his personal experiences and opinions about epilepsy in this book. His commentary reflects the true emotions and fears that patients deal with before the correct diagnosis is made. Despite his very busy schedule, his work and family commitments, his perspective of the disease was extremely helpful and is deeply appreciated.

Anuradha Singh, MD

I dedicate this book to my parents and my children.

Anuradha Singh, MD

# PART ONE

# *The Basics*

What is epilepsy?

What is a seizure?

How common is epilepsy?

What should I know about the brain to understand epilepsy?

Is epilepsy an inherited condition?

*More . . .*

# 1. I have seizures but do not think that I have epilepsy. What is epilepsy?

**Seizure**
An abnormal clinical behavior as a result of excessive excitation of brain cells.

**Neurons**
Building blocks of the brain made up of the cell body, the axon, and the dendrites.

**Epilepsy**
A neurological condition where a person has a tendency to have repeated seizures, more than two, that are unprovoked.

**Cortex**
The outer layer of an organ or other body structure.

**Paroxysmal**
A sudden outburst or eruption.

A **seizure** is defined as abnormal clinical behavior that is caused by excessive excitation of **neurons** (building blocks of the brain). **Epilepsy** seems to originate from an area of the brain called the **cortex** that is rich in neurons. The cerebral cortex is a convoluted structure on the surface of the brain. Seizures can be provoked or unprovoked. Epilepsy is defined as two or more unprovoked, recurrent **paroxysmal** seizures resulting in any abnormal clinical behavior or motor, sensory, psychic, or autonomic dysfunction. Seizures or epilepsy is not a specific disease but rather a symptom of abnormal function of the brain.

Epilepsy is a very common condition, with an incidence of 0.5% to 1.0%. The lifetime incidence of seizures is about 5% to 10%. This disease is most common at the two extremes of age. In fact, the incidence of epilepsy is highest in those who are younger than 5 years old and older then 65 years. About 300,000 people have their first convulsion each year. Of these, about 120,000 are under the age of 18 years. About 70,000 to 100,000 are children who are less than 5 years old and who have experienced fever-caused seizures. Approximately more than 300,000 school children through the age of 14 years have epilepsy. Males are slightly more prone to seizures than females. The incidence is higher in low socioeconomic groups and in blacks and is lower in whites. Approximately 10% of the American population will experience a seizure in their lifetime. Three percent of these will develop epilepsy by the age of 75 years. About 600,000 persons over the age of 65 years have epilepsy. The direct and indirect cost of epilepsy is estimated to be $12.5 billion.

The brain has two **hemispheres**: right and left. The right side of the brain controls motor and sensory functions of the opposite side of the body and vice versa. The cerebral hemispheres have the most complex three-dimensional configuration of all of the **central nervous system** divisions. The left hemisphere controls language functions (comprehension, expression, repetition, reading, and writing) in most patients. A band of nerve fibers called the **corpus callosum** connects the two hemispheres. The brain has different lobes: frontal, parietal, temporal, and occipital (Figure 1). The frontal and **parietal lobes** are the motor and sensory centers, respectively. The **temporal lobe** mediates a variety of sensory functions and is our memory and emotions center. The **occipital lobe** subserves visual perception. The lower part of the brain is called **brainstem**. The brainstem is in continuity with the spinal cord.

**The Basics**

**Hemispheres**
The brain consists of two of these (right and left).

**Central nervous system**
The portion of the vertebrate nervous system consisting of the brain and spinal cord.

**Corpus callosum**
A band of nerves that connects the two hemispheres.

**Parietal lobes**
The part of the brain that is involved in perceiving sensations.

**Temporal lobe**
The part of the brain that is involved in speech, language, memory, and in the perception of smell and taste.

**Occipital lobe**
The part of the brain that subserves visual perception.

**Brainstem**
The lower part of the brain.

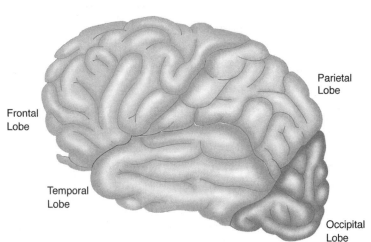

Parietal Lobe

Frontal Lobe

Temporal Lobe

Occipital Lobe

**Figure 1    Different lobes of the brain.**

**Cell body**

One part of a neuron.

**Axon**

Part of a neuron that conducts impulses away from the cell body.

**Dendrites**

Part of a neuron that conducts impulses from adjacent cells inward toward the cell body.

**Organelles**

Differentiated structures within a cell that perform specific functions.

**Synapses**

Contact points where the communication between the neurons is polarized.

**Neurotransmitters**

These are small-molecular-weight compounds that convey messages across a synapse.

**Glutamate**

An excitatory neurotransmitter.

**Gamma-aminobutyric acid**

A neurotransmitter that inhibits neuronal firing.

Seizures are the result of hyperexcitation and synchronization of firing neurons. Neurons are made of the **cell body**, the **axon**, and **dendrites**. The cell body contains the nucleus and other cellular **organelles**. The axon conducts information, and the dendrites and the cell body receive information from the other neurons. The communication between the neurons is polarized and occurs at sites of contact points called **synapses**. The neurons release chemical substances called **neurotransmitters** (chemical messengers of the brain). There are some excitatory and some inhibitory neurotransmitters in the brain. The main excitatory neurotransmitter is **glutamate**, and the main inhibitory neurotransmitter is **gamma-aminobutyric acid**. A tight balance is maintained between the excitatory and inhibitory neurotransmitters. Overactivation of glutamate and the inhibition of gamma-aminobutyric acid can cause excitation of the brain, thus resulting in seizures. This is an oversimplified explanation of the cause of seizures at a chemical level. Several other types of neurotransmitters exist in the brain. The interplay between the neurotransmitters plays a crucial role in controlling our memory and emotions.

Epilepsy can be the result of a structural abnormality such as brain tumors, stroke, and blood vessel anomalies of the brain. The prolonged lack of blood **(ischemia)** or oxygen **(hypoxia)** supply to the brain can result in selective neuronal loss. A certain population of neurons is very sensitive to hypoxia. One such example is the selective loss of cells in a structure called the **hippocampus** in the temporal lobe. The neuronal death results in scar formation, evident on the **magnetic resonance imaging (MRI)** of the brain. This is called **hippocampal atrophy** (Figure 2) or

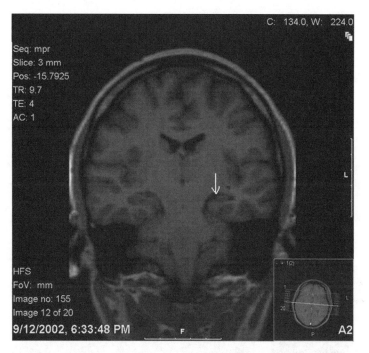

**Figure 2**  Left hippocampal atrophy: a common finding in temporal lobe seizures indicated by a white arrow. Left hippocampus is smaller compared to the right.

**mesial temporal sclerosis** (Figure 3). Some patients have certain risk factors for developing epilepsy; however, there are cases in which the cause of epilepsy cannot be determined. This is called **idiopathic epilepsy**. Sometimes the cause is highly suspected but cannot be determined despite careful search. This is called **cryptogenic epilepsy**.

Jared adds.....

*I had seizures for a long time before anyone realized that the cause was epilepsy (or even that they were seizures for that matter). When I found out that it was epilepsy, I was actually relieved because I finally had a name to put to what I had been experiencing.*

*Ischemia*

The prolonged lack of blood to the brain.

*Hypoxia*

The prolonged lack of oxygen to the brain.

*Hippocampus*

Part of the temporal lobe of the brain, that is involved in memory.

*Magnetic Resonance Imaging (MRI)*

A brain scan using magnetic field showing details of the structure of the brain in a three-dimensional way.

*Mesial temporal sclerosis*

Subtle scar seen in the temporal lobes in patients with temporal lobe epilepsy due to neuronal loss.

*Idiopathic epilepsy*

Epilepsy where the cause of the condition is not known but genetic factors are believed to be involved.

*Cryptogenic epilepsy*

Epilepsy where the cause of the condition cannot be determined.

The Basics

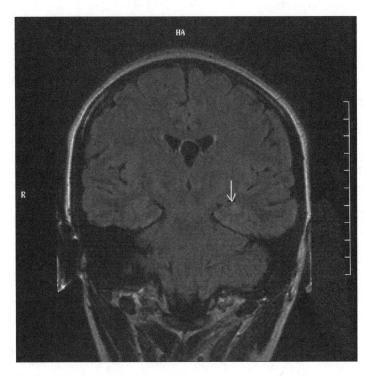

**Figure 3    Mesial temporal sclerosis: subtle scar tissue in the left temporal lobe as indicated above.**

## 2. I am not sure whether the episodes or spells I am having are seizures.

"Everything that shakes is not epilepsy." A patient or witness's good description can help the physician decide whether the recurrent events are truly seizures. The **vasovagal attacks**, **syncopal episodes**, or certain movement disorders can be easily confused with seizures. It is important to make that distinction so that patients are not subjected to any unnecessary long-term **antiepileptics**. Sometimes common metabolic abnormalities such as low or high glucose, low sodium, low calcium, or low phosphate or magnesium can provoke seizures. These abnormalities can be diagnosed by blood tests and corrected accordingly. In children, tics, migraines, night terrors, abdominal colic,

*Vasovagal attacks*

A temporary vascular reaction associated with rapid fall in heart rate and blood pressure.

*Syncopal episodes*

Transient loss of consciousness due to decreased blood supply to the brain.

*Antiepileptics*

Medications used to prevent the spread of seizures in patients with epilepsy.

and breath-holding spells are confused with seizures. Alcohol or recreational drug abuse may cause withdrawal seizures in some patients. Patients may get seizures after the use of certain prescription or over-the-counter drugs (brain stimulants, certain painkillers or **antibiotics**, cold or cough medicines, anesthetics, diet drugs, etc.) that lower the **seizure threshold**.

Jared adds…

*I had no name at all to put to what I was experiencing—a rise in the stomach, some confusion, and then I was fine. When I would go to the doctor as a child I would say, "I get a funny feeling in my stomach." He would say, "Have you tried some Pepto Bismol?" It took a* **neurologist** *to figure out that it was epilepsy.*

Vasovagal attacks precipitated by extreme fear, emotion, prolonged standing, or extremely hot temperatures are benign in nature. Some patients under extreme stress or anxiety can experience spells that simulate seizures but show no abnormality on the **electroencephalogram (EEG)**. These are classified as **nonepileptic seizures (NES)**. **Transient ischemic attacks** (ministrokes) are caused by brief ischemia (decreased blood supply of the brain). **Syncopal episodes** (fainting) can be related to dysfunction of the heart (Table 1). These spells may be preceded by light-headedness, blurring of vision, or cardiac symptoms (chest pain or pressure over the chest, palpitations, sweating) before a brief loss of consciousness. Near the end of the syncopal attack, patients may have brief stiffening or a few convulsive movements of extremities. This is called **convulsive syncope**. Syncopal episodes need a cardiac workup such as 24-hour monitoring of the heart rate (Holter monitoring), an ultra-

**The Basics**

**Antibiotics**
Drugs that fight infections.

**Seizure threshold**
A person's resistance to seizures that can be inherited. Patients with low seizure threshold have a higher propensity for seizures.

**Neurologist**
A physician who specializes in conditions of the nervous system.

**Electroencephalogram (EEG)**
Graphic representation of brain waves revealing the functional status of the brain.

**Nonepileptic seizures (NES)**
Seizures that are not caused by epilepsy.

**Transient ischemic attacks**
Ministrokes caused by brief ischemia.

**Convulsive syncope**
Brief loss of consciousness (syncope) associated with mild convulsions and stiffening.

**Table 1    Common Causes of Syncope**

- Vasovagal: fear, pain, situational
- Syncopal episodes after meals, cough, and urination
- Positional/orthostatic hypotension
- Cardiac
- No discernible cause

sound of the heart (echocardiogram), or a stress test. Sometimes sudden changes in posture can cause symptoms such as blurring or graying of vision before passing out, which can be a result of variability in the pulse or blood pressure. Symptoms result from maladaptation of the compensatory mechanisms in the heart or blood vessels as the posture is changed. A test called the Tilt-Table test can determine such irregularities in the pulse or blood pressure. Table 2 lists some of the recurrent episodes that should not be confused with epilepsy.

Jared adds...

*My experience is that under extreme stress (or even consistent mild stress) seizures were much more likely to occur.*

**Table 2    Recurrent Episodes That Imitate Epilepsy**

- Movement disorders: tics
- Sleep disorders: sleepwalking, night terrors, or nightmares
- Panic, anxiety, or rage attacks
- Breath-holding spells
- Migraine attacks
- Transient ischemic attacks
- Nonepileptic seizures
- Convulsive syncope
- Hypoglycemia (low glucose) or other electrolyte abnormalities

## 3. I did not have seizures in childhood, why did I have my first seizure at this age? How is this possible?

Epilepsy can occur at any age. It is most common in children and older people; however, the onset can occur at any age. Epilepsy can be broadly classified into two categories: partial and generalized (Table 3).

Patients with **generalized epilepsy** usually do not get any **auras**, as the **electrical epileptiform discharges**, resulting in seizures start from both hemispheres (originate in a generalized manner). Generalized epilepsy tends to occur at an earlier age. It is characterized by clinical changes indicating involvement of both hemispheres. Consciousness may be impaired at the onset. Motor manifestations are bilateral. Generalized epilepsy can have different seizure types, as listed in Table 3. Generalized epilepsy is further classified into primary and symptomatic generalized epilepsy, which are discussed later in this book. Patients with primary gener-

**The Basics**

*Generalized epilepsy*

Epilepsy characterized by different seizure types, such as, tonic-clonic, clonic, tonic, absence or myoclonic seizures. These are typically not preceded by any aura and show diffuse involvement of the brain on the EEG during the seizure.

*Auras*

Warnings before the seizure that a patient can recall.

*Electrical epileptiform discharges*

Abnormal excitation in the brain referred to as "epilepsy brain waves."

**Table 3   Classification of Seizures**

**Generalized Seizures**
- Absence (petit mal)
- Myoclonic
- Tonic–clonic
- Tonic
- Atonic
- Clonic

**Partial Seizures**
- Simple partial seizures
- Complex partial seizures
- Complex partial with secondary generalization

**Unclassified Seizures**

alized epilepsy may have a normal neurologic examination and a normal MRI of the brain. Further classification of **generalized seizures** is based on the clinical and EEG characteristics.

**Partial epilepsy** tends to occur at a later age. As the name suggests, the seizure starts from either the right or the left side of the brain. It may start in any lobe—frontal, parietal, temporal, occipital, or in the brainstem. Partial epilepsy most commonly originates from the temporal lobe.

Jared adds...

*My seizures began as a child and were always partial. When I was finally diagnosed, the electrical activity in my EEG was very characteristic of my type of epilepsy.*

## 4. I only had one seizure. Does that mean I will develop epilepsy?

About 50% of the people who have one unprovoked seizure will have another one, usually within the next 6 months. If someone had two unprovoked seizures, the chances of having a third one without antiepileptics are close to 80%. If your first seizure occurred at the time of an injury or infection in the brain, you double your chances of having a second seizure or of developing epilepsy. More seizures are also likely if your doctor finds neurologic deficits on examination or if any evidence exists of structural abnormalities on the MRI (such as tumors, vascular malformations, stroke, inborn brain developmental abnormalities, hemorrhage, or trauma to the brain). Patients with **lupus, multiple sclerosis, tuberous sclerosis,** or degenerative condi-

**Generalized seizures**

Abnormal electrical activity occuring simultaneously from both sides of the brain.

**Partial epilepsy**

Epilepsy originating from a part of the cortex.

**Lupus**

An autoimmune disorder causing inflammation in different organs, such as, the heart and kidneys, as well as the joints and blood vessels.

**Multiple sclerosis**

A neurodegenerative condition primarily involving the white matter of the brain.

**Tuberous sclerosis**

A neurological condition associated with seizures, mental retardation, and skin lesions. Multiple organs such as skin, heart, brain, kidneys, and eyes can be involved.

tions of the brain can also present with seizures. Sometimes the brain abnormality may not be obvious on the MRI because the abnormality is at a microscopic or chemical level (an imbalance of inhibitory and excitatory neurotransmitters). A certain kind of generalized epilepsy exists in which the brain MRI and neurological examination are normal. Some epilepsies are associated with skin manifestations, which have peculiar abnormalities on the brain MRI.

Another test that can help your doctor predict whether you have a predisposition to seizures is an EEG. Patients with epilepsy show hallmarks of abnormal brain excitation on their EEG. These are called epileptiform discharges (epilepsy brain waves). An abnormal EEG predicts the chances of relapse of seizures as well.

Jared adds…

*My EEG had the epileptiform discharges described. The seizures that I had as a child were very mild and, as such, were difficult to diagnose until I had a full EEG. As I got older, the frequency and severity of my seizures increased.*

## 5. Nobody in my family has epilepsy. Is epilepsy an inherited condition?

**Genetics** definitely influences some epilepsy. The **genes** that are responsible for epilepsy are expressed in a complex manner and have variable degrees of expression. Genetic and environmental factors probably play a role together. Sometimes the inheritance of a specific gene does not result in the disease, and therefore, some gene carriers are not affected. This is called **reduced penetrance**. At times, multiple genes may be responsi-

**Genetics**

Relating to genes.

**Genes**

Hereditary material composed of long strands of four molecules that determine the synthesis of proteins.

**Reduced penetrance**

The mutated gene effect is modified or reduced and does not always cause disease when present.

ble for developing epilepsy. On occasions, genetic heterogeneity (e.g., genetic and environmental factors [head trauma], together or alone) results in epilepsy. **Febrile convulsions,** juvenile myoclonic convulsions, and benign neonatal convulsions are some common epilepsy syndromes in which genes have been identified (Table 4).

**Febrile convulsions**

Convulsions seen with high fever.

Jared adds…

*Nobody in my family has epilepsy; thus, my family was confused about where it came from. I had some minor head injuries as a child (normal boy stuff), but none that could conclusively be linked as a cause.*

**Table 4    Genetically Inherited Epilepsy Syndromes**

- Benign neonatal convulsions
- Benign infantile convulsions
- Febrile seizures
- Childhood absence epilepsy
- Juvenile absence epilepsy
- Juvenile myoclonic epilepsy
- Nocturnal frontal lobe epilepsy
- Benign rolandic epilepsy

# PART TWO

# Risk Factors, Symptoms, and Seizure Types

What are the risk factors/triggers for epilepsy?

What are the different seizure types or epilepsy syndromes?

What are nonepileptic seizures?

*More . . .*

# 6. What are the risk factors for epilepsy?

There are various risk factors for epilepsy. In 70% of the cases, no apparent cause is identified. Starting at an earlier age, any problems at the time of birth such as decreased oxygen supply (hypoxia) to the brain can result into epilepsy. Certain inborn genetic/metabolic disorders are associated with a high incidence of epilepsy. These can be diseases associated with carbohydrates, protein, and fat metabolism. Few congenital disorders with skin manifestations are associated with epilepsy. One such example is tuberous sclerosis.

Some patients may experience seizures with high fever called **febrile seizures.** The onset of seizures occurs anywhere from 6 months until 4 years of age. Then the seizures may go into remission for several years, only to re-emerge during adulthood.

Some patients have a strong family history of seizures. Generalized epilepsy usually has a genetic origin. The genes that carry risks for epilepsy are variably expressed in a complex manner. After the age of 35 years, no definite genetic risk is involved. It is believed that the onset of epilepsy after 35 years of age is partial unless proven otherwise.

**Posttraumatic epilepsy**

Seizures resulting from head trauma.

**Meningitis**

Inflammation of the coverings of the brain.

**Encephalitis**

Inflammation of the brain tissue.

Previous head trauma with a loss of consciousness can lead to **posttraumatic epilepsy.** A prolonged period of loss of consciousness, a loss of memory about the trauma, skull fracture, and laceration of the coverings of the brain or bleeding in the brain have been shown to be definite risk factors for developing posttraumatic epilepsy. Any brain infections such as **meningitis** (inflammation of the coverings of the brain) or **encephalitis** (inflammation of the brain tissue) can also result in seizures.

Destruction of brain tissue as a result of stroke, tumor, or vascular malformation of the brain can also result in epilepsy. Special populations, which are listed in Table 5, are at a higher risk of developing epilepsy.

Jared adds...

*I had none of these symptoms and, therefore, am in the 70% for which no specific cause is identified. For my family, it was hard to understand how this could have just "happened," and there was a short period of time where at least one parent felt either responsible or blamed the other.*

## 7. Are there any triggers for epilepsy?

Specific stimuli trigger certain epilepsies. These are called **reflex epilepsies**. These are rare epilepsy syndromes and are usually classified as seizures that are provoked by a specific cause. Reflex epilepsies are rare and can be precipitated by stimuli such as flashing lights, startle, reading, writing, music, eating, or bathing in hot water (Figure 4).

**Reflex epilepsies**
Epilepsies that are triggered by specific stimuli.

The reflex epilepsies are mostly generalized or may have mixed features of both partial and generalized epilepsy.

**Table 5  Causes of Epileptic Seizures**

| | |
|---|---|
| • Congenital | • Tumors |
| • Perinatal (around birth) | • Trauma |
| • Genetic | • Toxic |
| • Idiopathic | • Vascular |
| • Infectious | • Degenerative |
| • Metabolic | |

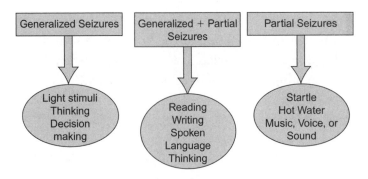

**Figure 4    Reflex epilepsy syndrome: Various stimuli.**

**Photosensitive epilepsy**

A form of epilepsy where seizures are triggered by flashing or flickering lights at particular frequencies.

Light triggers **photosensitive epilepsy**. Approximately 30% of the patients with generalized epilepsy exhibit **photosensitivity**. Individual patients are sensitive to certain frequencies or wave patterns of light. They may experience difficulty indulging in video games with a "wraparound" arrangement. A flickering sun glare along a tree-lined road may disturb patients while driving. Patients can wear polarized lenses or tinted glasses or cover one eye. Patients may view the computer or television screen from an angle. Liquid crystal display screens and low screen contrasts are preferred.

**Grand mal**

A sudden attack or convulsion characterized by generalized muscle spasms and loss of consciousness.

Certain pieces of music may precipitate musicogenic epilepsy. Reading epilepsy can present as brief jaw jerks before a **grand mal** seizure if a patient continues to read for a prolonged period. An interruption in reading can prevent seizures. Psychic processes such as chess playing, deep thoughts, hard political decisions, or mental arithmetic exercises can trigger seizures as well. Hot water epilepsy is a rare syndrome and is seen in certain parts of India. It can occur by pouring hot water over the head. Reflex epilepsies have a good prognosis overall. Seizures are infrequent and can be largely reduced by avoiding precipitating factors.

Jared adds…

*It seems as if all of the previously mentioned causes have produced seizures in me at one time or another; however, it is nearly impossible to say that there is one specific thing that always triggered a seizure. More often then not it was a combination of factors (lights, stress, loud music, intensity at work, etc.).*

## 8. I drink alcohol and rarely use recreational drugs. Can my seizures be related to drug or alcohol abuse?

Alcohol use is associated with increased seizures during the acute intoxication and withdrawal phases. Withdrawal seizures usually occur within 24 to 72 hours after the last ingestion of alcohol. Patients with alcohol withdrawal seizures should not be treated with **anticonvulsants**. Cessation of alcohol intake and referral to alcohol de-addiction rehabilitation programs are the mainstays of treatment.

**Anticonvulsants**
An antiepileptic drug used to treat seizures.

Recreational drugs can increase the risk of seizures by lowering the seizure threshold. Inhalation or ingestion of crack cocaine is associated with generalized seizures. Isolated spontaneous seizures produced by cocaine do not require any antiepileptics. Ecstasy and phencyclidine are frequently associated with seizures as well. On the other hand, marijuana and heroin have a low association with seizures; however, heroin may be mixed with contaminants that may lower the seizure threshold.

Jared adds…

*I am a recovering alcoholic (sober 13 years) and primarily smoked marijuana and drank. I had experience using hallucinogenic drugs. All of this occurred in my teens. I was never able to make a specific connection between drug/alcohol intake and the frequency of my seizures.*

## 9. I am not sure whether I am having small seizures. What should I look for?

The International League Against Epilepsy has classified different kinds of seizures. Seizures are broadly classified as partial (focal) or generalized. Some epilepsy may be "unclassified." Certain epilepsies are classified into syndromes. The "**epileptic syndromes**" take into account several features, such as similar age of onset and duration of epilepsy, severity, similar EEG findings, and associated clinical features. These syndromes stand out because of the constellation of signs and symptoms, and physicians can predict prognosis and response to certain anticonvulsants.

**Partial seizures** start from a focal area. Patients are able to recall the beginning of the seizure before losing consciousness. These are called auras, which are **simple partial seizures**. Patients are fully aware of their surroundings. The symptoms can vary depending on the area of the brain involved. The common auras that patients with **temporal lobe epilepsy** describe are a rising sensation in the stomach ("butterflies in the stomach or being in a roller coaster"), nausea, vomiting, feelings of familiarity (déjà vu), feelings of unfamiliarity (jamais vu), pleasant or unpleasant smell or taste, fear, anxiety, and dizziness (Table 6). Sometimes these episodes are wrongly diagnosed as anxiety or **panic attacks**;

**Partial seizures**

Seizures where the abnormal electrical activity begins in one part of the brain.

**Simple partial seizure**

A partial seizure where the person remains fully conscious but experiences unusual sensations.

**Temporal lobe epilepsy**

Epilepsy where the seizures originate in the temporal lobe of the brain. The seizures are usually complex partial seizures.

**Panic attacks**

Sudden onsets of panic with no apparent cause.

**Table 6    Different Kinds of Auras or Simple Partial Seizures**

Early Seizure Symptoms (Aura)

| Sensory/Thought | Emotional | Physical |
|---|---|---|
| • Smell | • Fear | • Dizziness |
| • Sound | • Anxiety | • Headache |
| • Taste | • Panic | • Lightheadedness |
| • Visual loss or blurring | • Pleasant feeling | • Nausea |
| • Déjà vu | | • Numbness |
| • Jamais vu | | |
| • Racing thoughts | | |
| • Forced thoughts | | |
| • Depersonalization | | |
| • Derealization | | |
| • Abdominal feelings | | |
| • Strange, hard to describe feelings | | |
| • Tingling feelings | | |

Seizure Symptoms (Ictal)

| Sensory/Thought | Emotional | Physical |
|---|---|---|
| • Blackout | • Fear | • Staring |
| • Confusion | • Panic | • Chewing/swallowing movements |
| • Muffling of sounds | | • Grinding teeth |
| • Electric shock feeling | | • Smacking lips |
| • Loss of consciousness | | • Racing heart |
| • Smell | | • Speaking difficulties |
| • Spacing out | | • Breathing difficulties |
| • Out-of-body experience | | • Vocalization (making sounds) |
| • Visual loss or blurring | | • Drooling |
| • Muffling of sounds/ deafness | | • Fluttering eyelids |
| | | • Tremors |
| | | • Sweating |
| | | • Eyes rolling up |
| | | • Falling down |
| | | • Inability to move |
| | | • Stiffening |
| | | • Incontinence to stools or urine |
| | | • Twitchings |
| | | • Convulsions |

(continued)

*19*

**Table 6    (continued)**

After-Seizure Symptoms (Postictal)

| Thought | Emotional | Physical |
|---------|-----------|----------|
| • Memory loss | • Confusion | • Physical injuries |
| • Writing difficulty | • Depression | • Difficulty talking |
| | • Fear | • Sleeping |
| | • Frustration | • Exhaustion/tiredness |
| | • Embarrassment | • Headache |
| | • Psychosis | • Nausea/vomiting |
| | | • Thirst |
| | | • Urge to urinate/defecate |

**Automatisms**

Automatic or altered behavior—typically occurring during a complex partial seizure—such as lip smacking, rearranging objects, chewing or swallowing movements, fumbling with clothing, and undressing.

**Frontal lobe epilepsy**

Seizures originating from frontal lobe(s).

**Nocturnal seizures**

Seizures that occur during sleep, usually at night.

**Absence seizures**

This is a generalized seizure involving a brief interruption of consciousness. The person briefly stares blankly and the eyelids may flutter. This is also called petit mal.

however, the seizures are unprovoked, stereotypical, and brief in duration. A typical partial seizure may last 1 to 3 minutes. Partial seizures starting from the motor or sensory cortex may include twitchings or jerky movements of the face, arm, or leg or a tingling/painful sensation on either side of the body. Patients may be confused or disoriented or may be seen wandering. Patients may stare blankly or have lip-smacking or chewing movements. Some patients may experience visual hallucinations and changes in hearing with the auras. Patients with temporal lobe seizures may exhibit purposeless movements of either hand called **automatisms**.

Patients with **frontal lobe epilepsy** have brief **nocturnal seizures** that are characterized by bizarre behavior. Patients exhibit strange behavior with lots of abnormal movements and vocalizations. These are brief and may be confused with nonepileptic seizures or sleep disorders.

Generalized seizures have their onset more diffusely in both hemispheres. Patients do not experience auras and have no recollection of their seizures. These can be of different kinds. Patients may have **absence seizures**.

These occur during childhood and tend to last less than 15 seconds. Children may have several staring episodes. Absence seizures are commonly called **petit mal** seizures. Children are often misdiagnosed with learning difficulties or attention deficit disorder. Childhood absence seizures start at the age of 7 years or as early as 4 years, and 80% of the children have resolution of their seizures by the age of 10 years.

**Myoclonic seizures** are brief sudden muscle contractions that are described as "muscle twitches." These tend to occur during morning hours or while going into sleep. Sometimes a series of myoclonic seizures may serve as a warning before a grand mal seizure. Patients may drop objects if myoclonic jerks involve the upper extremities. Myoclonic jerks involving the lower extremities may result in a fall with or without a loss of consciousness.

**Tonic seizures** and **atonic seizures** are other forms of rare generalized seizures that occur in children. Tonic refers to stiffening of the body, whereas atonia means loss of muscle tone. A sudden loss of muscle tone can cause a fall to the ground (so-called drop attacks). These children have to wear helmets to prevent serious head injuries from drop attacks. **Clonic seizures** are characterized by jerking movements of the body without stiffening. Tonic, atonic, and clonic seizures are usually encountered in children with developmental delays.

Jared adds…

*I have always had complex partial seizures. I knew something was happening to me, but I had no idea what. My father finally observed me having a seizure and watched*

**Petit mal**

Also called absence seizure.

**Myoclonic seizures**

Generalized seizures with brief jerks of a part of or the whole body.

**Tonic seizures**

Generalized seizures where the person's body becomes stiff and he or she may fall backward. The seizure usually lasts less than a one minute and recovery is rapid.

**Atonic seizures**

Generalized seizures causing sudden loss of muscle tone resulting in falls to the ground. Recovery is rapid, but the patient is at a risk of serious injuries to the head or other body parts.

**Clonic seizures**

Epileptic seizures characterized by jerking movements involving muscles on both sides of the body.

*me have symptoms that I had no idea were even there. The only way it was finally confirmed was with an EEG test.*

## 10. What are complex partial seizures?

**Complex partial seizures**

Partial seizures where the person's awareness is impaired.

Seizures with an alteration of consciousness are defined as **complex partial seizures**. This altered level of consciousness can vary from subtle detachment from the surroundings to a frank period of disorientation and confusion. Complex partial seizures are characterized by brief periods of confusion or disorientation; the individual may experience speech arrest, lip smacking, eye blinking, or purposeless movements of the hands (automatisms). Partial seizures can start from one **focus** and can spread to the other hemisphere. This is called a partial seizure with secondary generalization. This may look like a generalized (grand mal) seizure if the beginning of the seizure is not witnessed; however, a patient may be able to recall his or her aura. The aura is basically a simple partial seizure. A complex partial seizure can start as a simple partial seizure and then become a complex partial seizure before spreading to the other hemisphere. Complex partial seizures can, however, start with a state of confusion at their onset.

**Focus**

An identified area of the brain from which partial seizures arise.

Simple partial seizure . . . . . . . . . . . . . . . . . . . generalized tonic–clonic
Complex partial seizure . . . . . . . . . . . . . . . . . generalized tonic–clonic
Simple partial seizure . . . complex partial . . . generalized tonic–clonic

The symptoms experienced at the onset of the seizure may vary depending on what part of the brain they start from. For example, a patient may experience jerking movements of one side of the body if these originate from the motor areas of the brain. Tingling or an electrical or painful sensation may be felt if it arose from the sensory areas of the brain. Patients experiencing seizures from the temporal lobe often describe their auras as a dreamy state, a sudden rising surge in the body, butterflies in the stomach, an abnormal smell or taste, déjà vu (feelings of familiarity), or jamais vu experiences (feelings of unfamiliarity). The seizure starts from one focus or one lobe in the brain and may not remain confined to that particular lobe or that side of the brain. As the seizure spreads, the patients may experience different symptoms that are peculiar to the area involved.

This period during the seizure is called the **ictal** phase. The complex partial seizures may be followed by a phase called the postictal period. During the ictal phase, overexcitation of part of the brain or of the entire brain occurs. This overexcitation is followed by a partial or complete shutdown of the brain, resulting in weakness. Patients may have general weakness or may notice half-sided weakness. This could be motor or sensory deficits or speech or vision problems. This is called **Todd's paresis** (weakness). During the postictal phase, patients may feel totally fatigued. Their muscles may feel sore. Postictal headaches are common as well. Some patients go into a psychotic state after a flurry of seizures. This is called **postictal psychosis** and is more commonly seen with left-sided seizure focus and in patients with poorly controlled seizures.

**Ictal**
The period during a seizure.

**Todd's paresis**
Paralysis of temporary duration that occurs after a seizure.

**Postictal psychosis**
A state of psychosis occurring after seizure(s).

Jared adds…

*As someone who has experienced hundreds of complex partial seizures, the symptoms I have felt are actually in the reverse order from what is described here. I feel the aura that for me was a rising sensation in the stomach akin to very mild anxiety. Although it is true that I probably appear confused to an outside viewer, while the seizure is happening, detached from the world as I may have been, I felt quite aware in real time.*

*The confusion I have felt was only experienced afterward, at the end of the seizure, when I found myself trying to get my bearings.*

## 11. What is a tonic–clonic seizure?

**Tonic–clonic seizure**

This is a generalized seizure also called convulsion or grand mal.

**Incontinence**

Involuntary urination.

A **tonic–clonic seizure** is commonly known as a grand mal seizure. It is characterized by stiffening of all four extremities, followed by convulsive movements of arms and legs with or without tongue biting or urinary **incontinence**. Patients can suffer physical injuries, such as head trauma, lacerations, shoulder dislocations, or rib fractures. Patients can experience problems breathing and are at risk of aspiration. Tonic–clonic seizures can occur in patients with generalized or partial seizure. The only difference between the two is that with the generalized onset, the seizure onset involves both sides of the brain simultaneously, whereas a partial seizure may start from one focus but gradually or quickly spreads to involve both sides of the brain. The distinction between the two is important for choosing treatment options.

Jared adds…

**Video EEG**

A test involving simultaneous EEG and video recording.

*I have only had one known tonic–clonic seizure; it was observed in a controlled **video EEG** environment. I watched the tape afterward, and it pretty much happened as just described. Mine started as partial, and I bit my tongue, wet myself, and convulsed my body (so much so that my back hurt quite badly for a few weeks). The level of confusion I* *experienced afterward far exceeded what I normally felt with a complex partial seizure.*

## 12. What are nonepileptic seizures?

Nonepileptic seizures are episodes that are confused with seizures, but the EEG monitoring does not show any abnormal electrical activity in the brain. These are more common in females than males. Nonepileptic seizures are also seen in childhood and adolescence. Patients have episodes that tend to last longer than a typical seizure (minutes to hours) (see characteristic features listed in Table 7). Unlike seizures, nonepileptic seizures lack stereotypy. Symptoms are not intentionally produced or feigned. The episodes may be preceded by conflicts, external events, or emotional stress. Patients show different kinds of clinical behavior. Two categories of nonepileptic seizures exist: (1) attacks of motionless collapse and (2) attacks with motor phenomena. Patients either become motionless and unresponsive or can be partially responsive intermittently. They may resist eye opening or painful stimuli. They

**Table 7    Salient Features of Nonepileptic Seizures**

- Subconscious psychologic conflict
- Prolonged and variable duration
- Nonstereotypical
- Absence of facial clonic activity
- Rare urinary incontinence
- Tongue biting at the tip
- Postictal period usually absent
- Precipitated by emotional stress
- Coexisting psychiatric condition
- Physical injuries may occur
- Nonepileptic status may occur

may respond by gestures while being in a seizure. The attacks with motor phenomena are characterized by erratic thrashing movements of all four extremities with or without crying, screaming, back arching, or pelvic thrusting movements. The movements slowly build up, wax, and wane. Tongue biting, urinary incontinence, or self-injuries can occur during these attacks. Patients may have a history of psychiatric disorder or a history of physical or sexual abuse in the past. Some patients have epileptic as well as nonepileptic seizures. The video EEG is helpful in capturing the target events and distinguishing between the epileptic and nonepileptic seizures. The family can be informed about the nature of different episodes. About 20% of referrals to epilepsy centers are for nonepileptic seizures. Patients who are diagnosed with nonepileptic seizures need to be evaluated by a neuropsychiatrist and to receive regular psychotherapy and antidepressants.

## 13. What is juvenile myoclonic epilepsy?

**Juvenile myoclonic epilepsy** is one of the epilepsy syndromes with an onset usually in the teens. It is classified as generalized epilepsy, which is believed to be inherited. Patients may have three seizure types: grand mal, myoclonic, and absence. Absence seizures are the least common in this syndrome. The EEG reveals a typical pattern of abnormal electrical activity, described as polyspikes, and spike-wave activity at the frequency of 3 to 5 per second. Patients have a normal intelligence, a normal brain MRI, and a normal neurologic examination. About 90% of the patients are easily controlled with medications. Missing medications, alcohol

*Juvenile myoclonic epilepsy*

A syndrome with onset during teenage years and is characterized by absence, tonic-clonic, and myoclonic seizures.

provocation, sleep deprivation, and increased mental and physical stress are common precipitating factors for seizure relapse. Depakote, Lamictal, Mysoline, Klonopin, Topamax, Zonegran, Felbatol, and Diamox are some of the drugs that are used to treat this syndrome. Seizures are usually controlled with lower doses and **compliance** to antiepileptics or simple lifestyle modifications such as sleep hygiene and avoidance of alcohol.

**Compliance**

Taking medication as prescribed, (i.e. the correct dose at the correct times).

# PART THREE

# Diagnosis of Epilepsy

What tests are performed to confirm the diagnosis?

What is neuroimaging?

What is an electroencephalogram?

*More . . .*

## 14. What tests do I need to find out the cause for my seizures?

A good history that explores the nature of the event, the provoking or risk factors, and the presence or absence of an aura can help the physician find the diagnosis. This should be followed by a thorough general physical and neurological examination. Routine blood tests are done to exclude any electrolyte abnormalities or liver or kidney dysfunction. A good quality MRI of the brain and an EEG are the standard tests that are performed in patients with epilepsy.

An MRI of the brain excludes any structural abnormality that may be causing epilepsy. It can reveal several pathologies, such as tumors (benign or malignant), vascular abnormalities, hemorrhage in the brain, infections or inflammations of the brain, trauma sustained to the brain, and strokes. Sometimes the structural abnormalities on the MRI can be congenital. The neurons are laid down in a particular fashion. Neurons travel from the midzone toward the periphery during development. Defects may exist in this migration process determined by the genetic factors causing clumping of neurons in an abnormal location. Excessive or suboptimal proliferation of neurons results in abnormal brain tissue, which could be **epileptogenic**. During infancy or toddler years, some children suffer from febrile seizures. Some of these patients may reveal shrinkage or subtle scar tissue in their temporal lobes. These abnormalities are evident on MRI of the brain and are referred as **hippocampal atrophy** and **mesial temporal sclerosis**, respectively.

An EEG is the study of the brain waves. MRI and EEG are complementary to each other and provide a

**Epileptogenic**

Having the capacity to induce epilepsy.

**Hippocampal atrophy**

Shrinkage or volume loss of hippocampus.

great deal of information to your physician to help diagnose or confirm this condition.

Jared adds...

*I have had all of these tests (and then some). Probably the most useful thing that I did for my diagnosis, however, was to keep a journal of my seizures (a simple spreadsheet with the date, an approximate time, a brief description of what I remembered, and whether anyone else was there and what they saw).*

*I was shocked to realize how frequently I was actually having them. Because of the confusion that normally followed, until I started keeping records, I would tell the doctor that the frequency of my seizures was one to two episodes every 2 to 3 weeks or so. When I started to keep track, I realized that I was having three to four seizures a week!*

## 15. What is the difference between a CAT scan and an MRI of the brain? What are functional studies of the brain?

A **computerized axial tomography (CAT) scan** and an MRI are the pictures of the brain that can determine any structural abnormalities. The CAT scan can reveal traumatic brain injuries, hemorrhage, scar tissue, strokes, tumors, abnormal blood vessels or shrinkage of the brain (atrophy). The use of the CAT scan in the United States started in the early 1970s. The CAT scan exposes the patient to the risk of radiation, just like x-rays. The advantages of CT scanning include lower cost, easy availability in most places, and fast processing. It has lower resolution than an MRI. However, a

**Computerized Axial Tomography (CAT) scan**
A brain scan showing anatomy of the brain using x-rays.

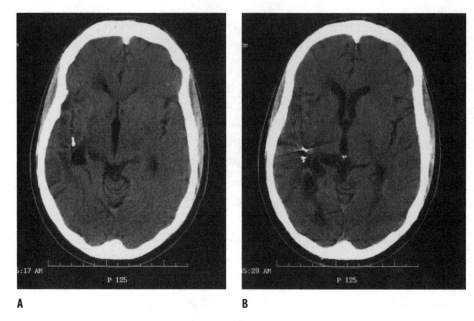

**A**        **B**

**Figure 5    A CAT brain with seizures secondary to acute stroke.**

CAT scan is not as good at discriminating between the brain's gray and white matter. CAT scan study is good to visualize hemorrhage or calcifications (Figure 5).

An MRI uses magnetic fields to align the spinning of atoms in water molecules. A brain image is created as small amounts of energy are released when the atoms relax to their normal state (Figures 6 and 7). An MRI is not so accessible, is more expensive, and takes a longer time to obtain pictures. An MRI has much better resolution compared with the CAT scan and gives a better view of the brainstem. Some MRI machines are much more powerful than others and produce higher quality images. A structural MRI provides information about the brain anatomy, whereas a functional MRI measures the rate of blood flow

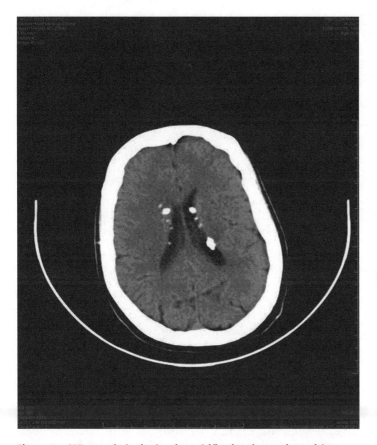

**Figure 6    CAT scan of a brain showing calcifications in a patient with seizures.**

through different parts of the brain, seeing how much light is absorbed by the brain structures.

Patients who have a metallic heart valve, metal in their body, a **vagal nerve stimulator**, a pacemaker, a bullet, or shrapnel in their body cannot have an MRI. Other hardware in the body, such as surgical plates, screws, staples, or pins used by orthopedists or neurosurgeons, pose no risk during an MRI. In cases of doubt, an x-ray can be obtained to find out the exact hardware used. Tooth fillings and braces are not affected by the magnetic field but can interfere with the quality of the

*Vagal nerve stimulator*

A small generator implanted in a person's chest. The generator stimulates the vagus nerve that may prevent the abnormal brain activity that gives rise to a seizure.

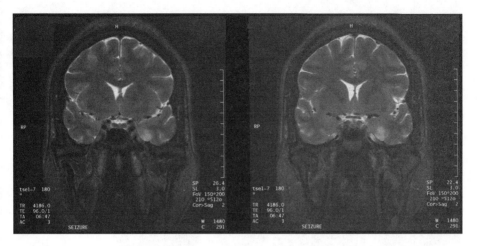

**Figure 7    MRI brain of a patient with seizures showing a brain tumor in the left temporal lobe.**

images of brain and facial bones. Some patients who are claustrophobic cannot tolerate a closed MRI. An MRI can be attempted under sedation in very young children or in patients suffering from mental retardation or claustrophobia. The conventional MRI is a cylindrical magnet in which the patient lies still for several seconds or few minutes at a time. An open MRI is another suboptimal but reasonable option if a patient is claustrophobic and sedation fails. An MRI is a painless test. Only the loud noises heard at different times can be bothersome.

Other neuroimaging methods show how the brain functions. A functional MRI measures the tiny metabolic changes that take place in an active part of the brain. This technique can delineate the motor, sensory, speech, language, or memory areas in the brain. This information can be of tremendous help before contemplating epilepsy surgery. In a functional MRI, the patient is asked to perform a task, and the metabolism in the area of the brain responsible for the task is studied.

**Single photon emission computerized tomography (SPECT)** measures blood flow through different parts of the brain. A small amount of low-level radioactive compound is injected into the arm. This radioactive material emits particles called **gamma rays** that are detected by the scanner. It takes about 10 to 20 minutes before the tracer reaches the brain. The number of particles emitted is directly proportional to the amount of blood flow in a region. This result is shown as a picture with different colors displaying different levels of blood flow. SPECT scans can be obtained during or between the seizures. During the seizure, there is increased blood flow (Figure 8) in the area that is believed to be the seizure focus. This study is called ictal (ictus = seizure) SPECT. In between the seizures, this area always reflects poor blood flow. This study is called interictal SPECT. The SPECT is a good study when EEG data are not clear cut and fail to determine what side of the brain is involved first in the seizure.

**Single photon emission computerized tomography (SPECT)**

A type of brain scan that gives information about the function and structure of the brain.

**Gamma rays**

Electromagnetic radiation emitted during radioactive decay that have an extremely short wavelength.

**Diagnosis of Epilepsy**

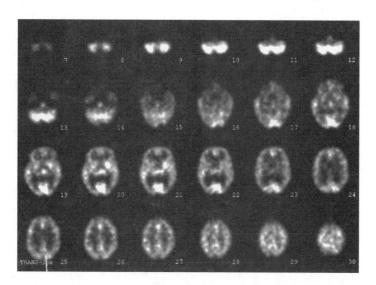

**Figure 8** SPECT scan showing increased blood flow on the right side most evident in images 24–29 in the bottom row.

This technique is very helpful when seizures begin outside of the temporal lobe and MRI scans fail to reveal any structural abnormality. SPECT scans are cheaper and more easily available. SPECT emits less radiation than a CT scan. Patients are encouraged to drink plenty of fluids to flush out any tracer.

**Positron emission tomography (PET)** shows how various areas of the brain use sugar (glucose) or oxygen. Just like SPECT, a very low, safe dose of a radioactive substance is injected into an arm, and the scanner measures circulation. It involves acquiring images by detecting **positrons**, which are tiny particles that are emitted from a radioactive substance. PET scans are brain maps that display different colors that show different levels of tissue or organ function. It determines what areas in the brain have higher or lower use of oxygen and sugar. This test can be helpful to identify the seizure focus in partial epilepsy. PET has a better resolution but is not readily available and is more expensive than SPECT.

The PET is an outpatient test. Patients are encouraged to drink water both before and after the test to flush the radioactive material. Patients should not eat for 4 hours before the scan. A radioactive substance is produced in a machine and is attached to a natural body compound such as glucose, water, or ammonia. Radioactivity is very short lived, and the radiation exposure is very low. The patient is given radioactive substance intravenously 30 to 60 minutes before finally being called for the scanning in a machine. Scanning takes an additional 30 to 45 minutes.

**Positron emission tomography (PET)**

A 3-dimensional brain scan that gives information about the function and structure of the brain.

**Positrons**

Electrically charged particles that have the opposite charge as electrons. They react with an electron to produce gamma rays.

**Magnetoencephalography (MEG)** identifies small magnetic fields generated by the brain's electrical patterns. Unlike EEG, there is less interference from the skull and other tissues. It uses 64 electrodes instead of 16, as in the standard EEG. The MEG provides greater accuracy because of less distortion of the electrical signals of the brain. This noninvasive technique is extremely helpful in identifying the areas of the brain that may be generating seizures or electrical activity in the brain. MEG pictures can be superimposed on MRI (Figure 9), which is called **magnetic source imaging (MSI)**. In patients who have brain tumors or other lesions, the MEG may be able to map the exact location of the normally functioning motor and sensory areas near the lesion. This information guides the neurosurgeon and helps to minimize the postoperative deficits. In patients with previous epilepsy surgery, the electrical field that the EEG measured may be distorted because of changes in the

*Magnetoencephalography (MEG)*

Noninvasive functional brain mapping which localizes electrical activity of the brain by measuring the associated magnetic fields emanating from the brain.

*Magnetic source imaging (MSI)*

Superimposition of MEG data on a magnetic resonance image (MRI).

**Diagnosis of Epilepsy**

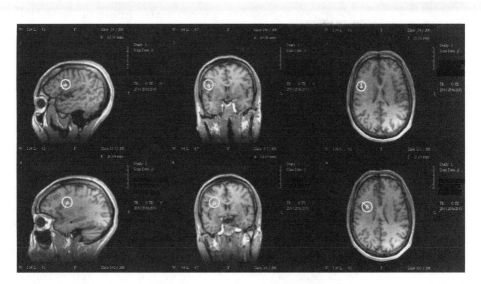

**Figure 9    MEG localizes epileptiform activity as indicated by circles.**

scalp and brain anatomy. An MEG may be a useful tool in complicated cases when the abnormality on the brain MRI and the seizure focus localization on EEG do not match each other.

Patients are asked not to eat after midnight. They can take their medicines with little sips of water. Patients should not have any contraindications of MRI. Sometimes an MEG is done under sedation. EEG electrodes are glued on the head. Three small coils are attached to the forehead, and two other coils are attached to the earplugs. The electrodes and coils are plugged into sensors. The stimulation tests may be performed with little plastic sensors on the fingers or feet. Patients may be shown different colors on a video. These stimulation tests can delineate the motor, sensory, or visual sensory cortex.

**Magnetic resonance spectroscopy**

Detection and measurements of resonant spectra of molecules (metabolites) in a tissue sample.

The **magnetic resonance spectroscopy** uses technology that is similar to MRI, but it uses a three times stronger magnet compared with conventional MRI. This study also reflects brain functioning by measuring the concentration of several chemicals and their breakdown products in normal and diseased areas of the brain. It is an evolving technique, which is still in its infancy. Its interpretation also needs expertise.

**Diffusion tensor imaging (DTI)**

Measures the movement of water in the brain.

**Diffusion tensor imaging (DTI)** measures the movement of water in the brain, detecting areas where the normal flow of water is disrupted. A disrupted flow of water indicates where there could be an underlying abnormality. If the location of the abnormality indicates that surgery may be possible, presurgical evaluation will be considered. This method of testing is new—only a few patients have had epilepsy surgery after a diffusion tensor imaging scanner detects an abnormality.

Jared adds…

*I have had an MRI and a PET scan (the PET to help me qualify for surgery). The MRI turned out nothing obvious, however, and thus, it was primarily the predictability of my EEG that was used in my diagnosis.*

## 16. What is an EEG?

A standard EEG is an outpatient test. Like the **electrocardiogram**, the EEG is the rhythm of your brain. An EEG is state dependent and dynamic and is very sensitive to any artifacts. EEG exhibits different kind of frequencies during wakefulness, drowsiness, and sleep stages. It takes 40 to 60 minutes to complete a standard study. An **epileptologist** has expertise in reading the EEG.

**Electrocardiogram**
The curve traced by an electrocardiograph.

**Epileptologist**
A neurologist who specializes in epilepsy.

Electrodes (usually 16) are placed in an orderly manner over the surface of the scalp with the help of special removable glue (Figure 10). The electrical activity

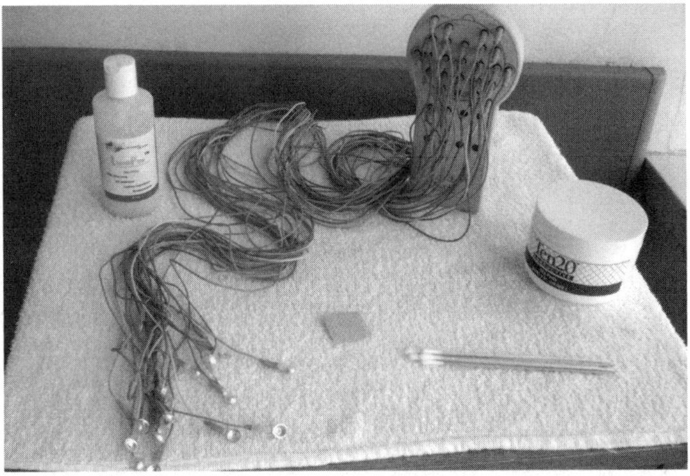

Figure 10    Scalp electrodes used to record EEG tracings.

is recorded from the surface of the brain, and this cerebral signal is converted to a digital signal and displayed on a computer (Figure 11) that is equipped with specialized monitor display software. There are two activation procedures done during EEG recordings; these are called **hyperventilation** and **photic stimulation**. The EEG technician asks the patient to do deep breathing exercises for 5 minutes and flashes strobe light of different frequencies (2 to 20 Hertz) during these activation procedures. A sleep-deprivation study (patients are asked to sleep less the night before) increases the yield of the study.

In the "take-home EEG" (24- or 48-hour study), a technician attaches electrodes, and the patient goes home with a portable computer. The patient maintains a logbook about the activities such as eating and drinking and also pushes the button if he or she experiences any auras or a typical seizure. Digitrace and **ambulatory EEGs** are prolonged and can be done at home. These are useful alternatives to video EEG,

*Hyperventilation*

Rapid, deep breathing; this technique may provoke epileptiform waves or seizures (especially petit mal seizures) during EEG recording.

*Photic stimulation*

Stimulation of the brain by flashing light or alternating patterns of light and dark.

*Ambulatory EEGs*

Portable type of EEGs that allow the electrical activity of the brain to be recorded over a period of several hours or days.

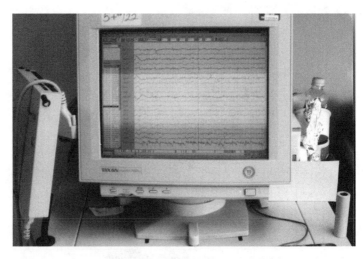

**Figure 11  Computer recording digital EEG.**

because the patient does not have to be in the hospital. Digitrace can be done with or without a video. The patients with daily seizures or other unclear episodes who are unable or unwilling to go to the hospital and are more comfortable in their own surroundings can be monitored at home. Such longer EEG recordings provide more useful information than routine office EEGs before discontinuing the medications or resorting to driving. A normal EEG background has mixed frequencies during wakefulness and sleep (Figure 12).

Patients with epilepsy show hallmarks of epilepsy. These abnormal epilepsy brain waves are called **epileptiform discharges** (Figure 13) and stand out from the normal background. Activation procedures irritate the brain and induce abnormal findings in certain types of epilepsy. Petit mal seizures or absence seizures can be induced by deep breathing exercises. Certain primary generalized epilepsies are photosensitive to light. Deep breathing exercises are avoided if

**Epileptiform discharges**

Abnormal waves in an EEG in patients with epilepsy that indicate signs of excitation in the brain.

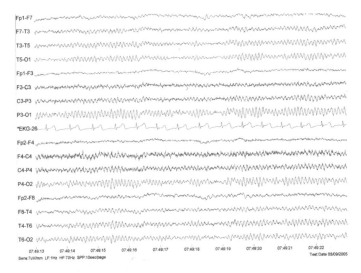

**Figure 12    Normal EEG tracings in an awake, relaxed patient.**

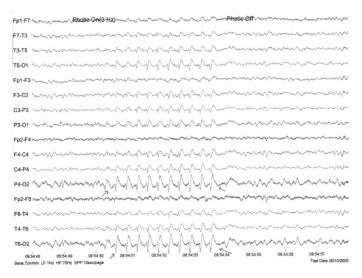

**Figure 13    EEG showing occipital spikes (indicated by arrows) with maximal electrical field in the occipital electrodes $O_2 > O_1$**

the patient has underlying asthma or other respiratory or heart conditions. Hyperventilation is not done in patients older than 65 years.

Jared adds...

*I have had both types of EEGs (digitrace and ambulatory). Over the years I have had dozens of ambulatory EEGs. The digitrace didn't turn up any new information, but the experience of walking around with all of that wiring was certainly interesting.*

## 17. I have had several normal EEGs; however, I have seizures. How is this possible? I do not understand this.

A normal EEG does not support or refute the diagnosis of epilepsy. An outpatient EEG is normal in 50% of the patients with seizures. These EEGs were not obtained during the time of seizures. Sometimes patients with generalized seizures may have normal EEGs in between the seizures. Patients with frontal lobe epilepsy may not show any abnormal epileptiform discharges.

## 18. What is an inpatient video EEG test?

An inpatient video EEG test is done at epilepsy monitoring units. The electrodes are placed on the scalp, similar to the standard EEG, but are left on the scalp for a few days. This test records both awake and sleeping EEGs. Sometimes, epilepsy brain waves are seen in different stages of sleep. Such patients may have a normal awake EEG. The yield of the video EEG is higher because it is a prolonged monitoring and also includes sleep records. The awake outpatient EEG may fail to pick up epilepsy brain waves.

Patients are admitted to the epilepsy monitoring unit to understand the nature of their paroxysmal episodes. The average length of stay is 3 to 5 days, although it could be longer. It confirms the diagnosis of epilepsy in a more objective manner. Depending on the location and type of abnormal epilepsy brain waves, epileptologists are able to classify the kind of epilepsy—partial or generalized. This test helps physicians understand the patient's prognosis and the impact of epilepsy on the functioning of the brain. It also helps them pick the most suitable drug option for the kind of seizures a patient has.

The epileptologists look at the abnormal behavior of the patients closely on the video; this helps them to determine whether these are seizures. The simultaneous EEG recordings can pinpoint from what part of the brain the seizure starts. The events that do not look like seizures and show no change on the EEG during the event are referred as nonepileptic events. The nonepileptic nature of the episodes can be confirmed, thereby obviating the need to use antiepileptics in the future.

Jared adds...

*My video EEG lasted over 10 days. I cannot emphasize how important it is to have the support of friends and family (especially friends) during this time. I was amazed at how many people were willing to visit just to bring me some nonhospital food or to hang out for a few minutes to shoot the breeze. Don't be afraid to ask for help!*

## 19. Will you lower my antiepileptics to capture seizures during hospitalization? My seizures occur randomly. What if I do not have any seizures during the hospital stay?

If no spontaneous seizures occur, the medications are frequently lowered in the epilepsy monitoring units. This is especially done for patients who have failed several medications in the past. If all seizures are stereotyped and EEG reflects a single seizure focus, epilepsy surgery becomes an option in patients with suboptimal control. Patients with poorly controlled seizures or a history of **status epilepticus** are frequently admitted to the epilepsy monitoring unit for safer change or adjustment of antiepileptics. Patients are weaned from their old antiepileptics in a safer setting, and a new drug is slowly introduced. Therefore,

**Status epilepticus**

Seizures continuing for a prolonged time, usually more than 30 minutes, without returning to baseline.

inducing seizures is not always the primary goal for admission to an epilepsy monitoring unit.

Several activation procedures, including sleep deprivation, hyperventilation, and photic stimulation, are done during epilepsy monitoring unit admission. It is true that sometimes seizures may not be captured despite all this during a brief hospital stay, but longer EEG recordings are much more informative than a routine outpatient EEG. The majority of epilepsy waves are seen during different stages of sleep, upon awakening, or in the transition from wakefulness to sleep. The abnormalities determine the kind of epilepsy that the patient has. It indirectly gives a quantitative measurement of abnormality in the EEG. The longer study helps the physician determine the prognosis and effects of antiepileptics on the EEG. Sometimes serial normal inpatient EEG recordings also raise doubts about the correct diagnosis. It also helps determine the best therapeutic options and guides the optimal doses of antiepileptics. Sometimes patients are admitted for safer medication adjustments. Medication adjustment is difficult as an outpatient for those with very frequent seizures or for those who are at risk of status epilepticus. Patients are admitted for presurgical evaluation when at least two or three of their typical seizures are captured before the epilepsy surgery. In difficult cases, ictal SPECT is obtained as well. Neuropsychologic and neuropsychiatry evaluations are routinely done as a part of the presurgical evaluation.

Jared adds...

*I was very frustrated in the hospital during my monitoring. I was used to having three to four seizures a week, and after being in the hospital, off my medication, it took 10 days for me to finally have a seizure.*

## 20. What is a comprehensive epilepsy center?

**Neurology**

The medical science that deals with the nervous system and disorders affecting it.

**Neuroradiologists**

Specialists who use imaging devices and substances to study the brain.

**Neurosurgeons**

Surgeons that carry out surgery for the treatment of conditions of the nervous system.

**Neuropsychiatrists**

Doctors who specializes in neurological conditions that are producing psychiatric symptoms.

**Neuropsychologists**

Doctors who specializes in the relationship between the brain and how individuals think and behave.

**Intracranial EEG recording**

EEG recording from intracranial electrodes.

**Ketogenic diet**

A high-fat diet that is sometimes used to treat severe epilepsy in children.

Epilepsy is a subspecialty of **neurology** and requires special training in understanding and reading brain waves (EEG) and taking care of patients with epilepsy. The subspecialists are called epileptologists. Comprehensive epilepsy center professionals take care of patients with epilepsy. It is a multidisciplinary team approach by epileptologists, **neuroradiologists**, **neurosurgeons**, **neuropsychiatrists**, **neuropsychologists**, EEG technicians, nurses, nurse practitioners, nutritionists, and social workers. Comprehensive epilepsy programs were created in the 1970s, with the National Institutes of Health providing funding. Comprehensive epilepsy programs typically consist of three areas: research, education, and direct services. These also address the psychosocial issues that are associated with epilepsy. Such centers have state-of-the-art technology that helps physicians to decide the drug options for the kind of seizures that the patient is suffering from. If medical treatment fails, patients are admitted for presurgical evaluation. Seizures are captured to determine the seizure focus. The presurgical evaluation aims to maximize the seizure control and minimize the postoperative deficits. Patients who opt for epilepsy surgery are admitted as well. Patients return for video EEG recording after the placement of electrodes directly over the surface of the brain. This is called an **intracranial EEG recording** (compare scalp recording). Brain mappings are performed in patients who are undergoing epilepsy surgery.

Patients are admitted for the initiation of a **ketogenic diet** under the supervision of a nutritionist. Patients with nonepileptic seizures are diagnosed in the comprehensive epilepsy center and are referred for psychotherapy to a neuropsychiatrist. Patients with a cluster of seizures are admitted for stabilization of seizures and medication adjustments.

SPECT studies are performed in the epilepsy monitoring unit as well. The radioactive material is injected intravenously at the beginning of the seizure to obtain an ictal SPECT. Ictal SPECTs are performed in patients when an EEG fails to determine the seizure focus clearly, but the behavior during the seizure suggests a partial focus.

Jared adds...

*I saw a neurologist for almost 10 years before being referred to the comprehensive epilepsy center. Keeping a journal of my seizures and trying multiple combinations of medication without success led to the referral.*

*Being seen at the comprehensive epilepsy center was very important, especially after my successful surgery, when I became unpredictably emotional. I was able to see a neuropsychiatrist who had a specialty in what I was going through.*

# PART FOUR

# Treatment and Its Side Effects

What is the first aid for seizures?

What are antiepileptics?

What are their side effects?

*More...*

## 21. What should be done in the event of a seizure? Should I call 911?

The first aid for seizures requires staying calm. The witnesses should prevent any injury during a loss of consciousness. During a grand mal seizure, the patient should be turned toward his or her left side to avoid the risk of aspiration. Try to keep onlookers away. Do not put anything in the person's mouth. Never give anything by mouth until the person is fully alert. Pay attention to the length of the seizure. Most of the seizures last for 1 to 3 minutes. If the seizures last longer than 5 minutes, call 911. Make sure that the airway is maintained, that the person is able to breathe, and that he or she is not turning blue for a long time. The patient should not be restrained. During or immediately after the seizures, patients are confused or disoriented and may turn violent if restrained. Be sensitive and supportive. It is not unusual for patients to sleep or be unresponsive for 15 to 30 minutes after a prolonged grand mal seizure. Patients who have frequent and prolonged seizures, a cluster of seizures, or a previous history of status epilepticus should be provided with rectal Diastat for immediate cessation. First aid for seizures is listed in Table 8.

## 22. What is the treatment for epilepsy?

Several studies have shown that a single unprovoked seizure does not warrant any treatment. If the patient has had more than two unprovoked seizures, the chance for a third seizure if left untreated is close to 80%. The seizure medications are called antiepileptics. A single drug is tried to control seizures.

**Table 8    First Aid for Seizures**

- Protect from nearby hazards
- Loosen clothing
- Protect from head injury
- Turn the patient to the left to keep the airway clear
- Never put anything in the mouth
- Do not try to hold the tongue, as it can be swallowed
- Time the seizure
- Do not restrain the patient
- Inform the patient that he or she had a seizure after the seizure is over
- Call the ambulance if prolonged seizure, cluster, or patient got injured, is diabetic, or is pregnant

The majority of patients never have a second seizure. Sometimes there may be tolerance problems or **allergic reactions**. **Monotherapy** is tried at maximal tolerated doses before adding a second drug to the regimen. About 20% to 30% of the patients are refractory to any medical treatment. If two correctly chosen antiepileptics fail, the chances that a third drug will make the person seizure free are less than 5%. These patients are considered to have **medically refractory seizures**. The presurgical evaluation should be done to determine whether these patients are good surgical candidates. The seizure focus can be removed by surgery if it is a discrete focus. This is called surgical resection of seizure focus. If there are multiple foci, a pacemaker-like device called a vagal nerve stimulator can be implanted surgically to reduce the frequency of the seizures. Some other surgical choices are also available for selected seizure types or refractory cases, as discussed in later sections of this book.

**Allergic reactions**

Allergic reactions are side effects that occur because an individual is sensitive to the drug. One example is rash.

**Monotherapy**

The use of one drug only in the treatment of any medical illness.

**Medically refractory seizures**

Those seizures that are not completely controlled by medical therapy alone as monotherapy or in combination.

*Treatment and Its Side Effects*

## 23. What drugs are you going to use? What are the side effects of these drugs?

The drugs that are used to treat epilepsy are called antiepileptics or anticonvulsants. The diagnosis of epilepsy must be correct and should be confirmed before starting treatment. The risk of recurrence of seizures must be genuine. The decision of treatment depends on the type of seizures, the severity, the timing and duration of the seizures, and the precipitating factors. It is important to have a clear understanding of why the treatment is necessary and the potential side effects of different antiepileptics. The right drug is chosen at the lowest dose to avoid adverse effects while aiming for seizure freedom. The goal of treatment for epilepsy is "seizure freedom, no side effects, and a good quality of life."

Some side effects (listed in Table 9) are common to all antiepileptics. The side effects can be either dose dependent or idiosyncratic. The dose-dependent side effects are related to the concentration of the drug in the brain or bloodstream. There are some specific untoward effects of different drugs. "Idiosyncratic" side effects are rare and potentially serious or life threatening (Table 10). These usually tend to occur in the initial few months of taking a medicine and are not dose related. Some antiepileptics can cause acute liver failure and bone marrow suppression in only a few patients. The choice of antiepileptics is based on the seizure type, the EEG pattern, the effectiveness against seizures, and the patient's tolerance. You must notify your physician of this if seizure control is not satisfactory or if the side effects are intolerable. Seizure patterns may change; this may require changes in your

**Table 9    Common Adverse Effects of Antiepileptics**

- Fatigue
- Sleepiness
- Lack of focus
- Slow thinking and processing of information
- Mood changes, depression
- Appetite changes
- Weight changes (weight gain or weight loss)
- Nausea, vomiting, constipation, or diarrhea
- Dizziness and balance problems
- Tremors
- Sexual dysfunction

medications. For example, during pregnancy, after menopause, during adolescence, or after age 65, changes in the body can alter the metabolism and clearance of drugs from the body. The handling of the medications in liver and kidney diseases may change, thus demanding different medications or a change in their doses. Two patients with the same seizure type and same EEG pattern may have a different response to the same antiepileptic medications. The drugs may

**Table 10    Idiosyncratic Side Effects of Antiepileptics**

- Rash (can be life threatening)
- Prolonged fever
- Liver failure or inflammation of liver
- Bone marrow suppression
- Aplastic anemia (low white and red blood cell counts and low platelets)
- Severe sore throat/oral ulcers
- Easy bruising
- Swollen glands
- Increased seizures
- Stevens-Johnson syndrome

Treatment and Its Side Effects

*53*

work for one and may not work at all for another patient or cannot be continued because of intolerable side effects. Therefore, the choice has to be individualized for each patient. Newer antiepileptics are better tolerated than the old ones (Table 11). Tolerance to antiepileptics varies from patient to patient. It is important to read about the drug you have started to take, to be aware of the side effects, and to bring to your physician's notice on your next office visit. Broadly speaking, most medicines are tolerated well. If you feel any symptoms when starting or changing the dose of the medications, then the medicine is likely the cause. Making these observations more closely is even more important in patients who are taking more than two or three medications for their seizures. The common side effects can involve any organ system, as listed in Table 12.

*Nervous system:* The adverse effects on the brain include sleepiness, tiredness, and feeling groggy or dizzy. Patients may experience balance problems or double vision. Cer-

**Table 11    Old- and New-Generation Antiepileptics**

Old Antiepileptics

| | |
|---|---|
| • Bromides | • Valium |
| • Phenobarbital | • Tegretol |
| • Dilantin | • Depakote |
| • Trimethadione | |

Newer Antiepileptics (after 1993)

| | |
|---|---|
| • Felbatol | • Keppra |
| • Neurontin | • Zonegran |
| • Lamictal | • Extended release Tegretol |
| • Topamax | • Extended release Depakote* |
| • Gabitril | • Extended release Dilantin |
| • Trileptal | • Rectal Diastat gel |
| | • Lyrica |

*Extended Release = once-a-day treatments that result in smoother blood levels

**Table 12   Effects of Antiepileptics on Multiple Organs**

- Liver: increased liver enzymes, liver failure (rare)
- Gastrointestinal: nausea, vomiting, diarrhea
- Kidney: stones
- Skin: thickening and coarsening of skin, hair growth or hair loss, acne, rash
- Eyes: double vision or blurring of vision
- Connective tissue: gum hypertrophy, contractures, lupus-like syndrome
- Ovaries: cyst formation, irregular or cessation of menstrual cycle
- Bones: thinning of bones (osteopenia and osteoporosis)
- Blood: low sodium and bicarbonate levels, low white blood cells, and low platelets

tain medications are believed to be more activating, such as Felbatol and Lamictal, and may be associated with trouble initiating or maintaining sleep. The ability to think clearly (often described as a "mental fog") may be affected. This is more common with older medicines (Dilantin, Tegretol, phenobarbital, and Mysoline), but it is also seen with newer medicines (Topamax and Zonegran). The cognitive problems can be due to antiepileptics, increased epileptiform activity, or ongoing seizures in the brain. Medications may cause irritability and mood changes. Phenobarbital is associated with cognitive side effects, learning difficulties, hyperactivity, and irritability, especially in children. Keppra can cause behavioral changes as well; however, mood swings are common with Tegretol, Dilantin, Mysoline, and phenobarbital. Lamictal is an activating drug and may precipitate or worsen the anxiety, headaches, or insomnia. The chronic use of antiepileptics, especially Dilantin, can cause **cerebellar atrophy**, resulting in balance and coordination problems. Some of the old antiepileptics can also cause neuropathy (involvement of the peripheral nerves of the body). This condition manifests as pins and

*Cerebellar atrophy*
Shrinkage of the lower part of the brain called the cerebellum, which is important for the coordination of movement and balance.

*55*

needles sensation in the feet and hands (called **paresthe-sias**). Patients on Topamax may experience paresthesias as well. Newer antiepileptics are overall better tolerated than the older antiepileptics. Some of the common side effects of old and new antiepileptics are listed in Table 13.

*Skin and mucosa:* Antiepileptics can cause several skin changes. Oral mucosa may be involved as well. For example, Dilantin can cause gum bleeding, overgrowth of gum tissue, hair growth, or coarsening of the skin. Older medications, such as phenobarbital and Myso-line, may be associated with connective tissue changes or contractures of the skin. Depakote can cause hair loss. These side effects may be particularly unaccept-able to female patients. Allergic reactions can occur with the use of antiepileptics. A rash associated with itching is usually benign. Contact your physician right

**Paresthesias**

A sensation of prick-ing, tingling, or creeping on the skin.

**Table 13   Adverse Effects of Antiepileptics**

Old Antiepileptic Drug Side Effects
- Phenobarbital and Primidone: irritability, depression, contractures, cognitive side effects
- Dilantin: hair growth, swollen gums, acne, low white blood cells, liver enzyme elevation
- Tegretol: tiredness, double vision, balance problems, nausea, headache, diarrhea, low white blood cells
- Depakote: weight gain, hair loss, tremor, Parkinsonism effect

New Antiepileptic Drug Side Effects
- Neurontin: weight gain, sedation, dizziness
- Topamax: weight loss, loss of appetite, kidney stones, difficulty thinking, tingling and numbness of fingers and toes, decreased sweating and heat regulation
- Zonegran: weight loss, sedation, loss of appetite, kidney stones
- Keppra: mood and behavioral changes
- Trileptal: nausea, vomiting, retching, low sodium
- Lyrica: dizziness, imbalance, tiredness, sleepiness, dry mouth, increased appetite, weight gain, euphoria (feeling "high").

away if a rash appears. Sometimes a consult with the dermatologist may be required. Few antiepileptics may have to be increased slowly to eliminate the risk of rash. One such example is Lamictal. The risk of rash with Lamictal is greater in children or in patients who are also using Depakote.

*Bone:* Older medicines carry a higher risk of **osteoporosis** and need to be changed if the bone densitometry (DEXA) scan shows frank osteoporosis. Osteoporosis is associated with a higher risk of vertebral or hip fractures.

**Osteoporosis**
A condition characterized by decrease in bone mass with decreased bone density and enlargement of bone spaces producing brittleness.

*Sex hormones:* In women, certain medications interfere with the menstrual cycles. The antiepileptics also lower the efficacy of oral contraceptives and cause difficulty in conceiving or cystic changes in the ovaries. Some anti-epileptic drugs have been known to cause polycystic changes in the ovaries, which may be associated with irregular menstrual cycles, obesity, high androgen levels, and lactation. Patients with all of these symptoms should have hormonal assays and an ultrasound of the ovaries. Antiepileptics can cause lowering of serum testosterone levels.

*Weight changes:* Closely follow any weight changes as patients start taking antiepileptics (Table 14). You may notice weight gain (with Depakote, Neurontin, or Tegretol) or weight loss (with Topamax, Zonegran, Felbatol, or ketogenic diet). Some drugs, such as Lamictal, may be weight neutral.

**Table 14  Antiepileptic Drugs and Body Weight Changes**

| Weight Gain | Weight Loss | Weight Neutral |
| --- | --- | --- |
| Tegretol | Felbatol | Lamictal |
| Depakote | Topamax | Keppra |
| Neurontin | Zonegran | Dilantin |
| Sabril | | |
| Lyrica | | |

*Kidneys:* The chance of kidney stones is increased with the use of Topamax, Zonegran, a ketogenic diet, or Diamox. This complication is rare; however, patients with a family history of kidney stones or who are taking a combination of these medications may be particularly prone to developing this complication. Some drugs may be primarily excreted by the kidneys, such as Keppra and Neurontin. All antiepileptic doses may need to be adjusted in patients with kidney dysfunction.

*Liver:* Patients on antiepileptics frequently show a mild elevation of liver enzymes. Elevation of enzymes more than three times may be worrisome and may require choosing other antiepileptics. Liver failure is one of the very rare idiosyncratic side effects of antiepileptics. Depakote is avoided in children who are less than 2 years of age because of immaturity of the liver.

*Changes in blood chemistry:* Aplastic anemia is a rare complication of antiepileptic drugs. This can be life threatening, as bone marrow suppresses the formation of all red and white blood cells and platelets. More commonly, low sodium (Tegretol, Trileptal), low white blood cell (Tegretol, Dilantin, Trileptal), low platelet count (Depakote), and a mild elevation of liver enzymes are seen. Most of the antiepileptics can lower the levels of thyroid hormones. The side effects may prove to be beneficial in some patients. Migraine, mood disorders, anxiety, or depression are common in patients who are suffering from epilepsy. Depakote and Topamax have proven efficacy in migraine. Lamictal, Tegretol, or Depakote act as mood stabilizers and may prove useful in bipolar or mood disorders.

Jared adds...

*I have felt very few side effects from antiepileptic medications. The ones I have had are as follows: I had an uneven sensitivity to the sun (resulting in splotchy tanning), and on Topamax, I lost a lot of weight.*

## 24. I get frequent headaches. Are they related to the seizures or medications?

Epilepsy and migraine can coexist. These two chronic disorders share some common features. Both are episodic and may have some overlapping features creating a diagnostic dilemma. Individuals with one disorder are twice as likely to suffer from the other disorder. Both occur at an increased prevalence, but the two can occur independently. Both can get worse just before or during menstrual periods in women (**catamenial migraine** and **catamenial epilepsy**). A migraine attack (migralepsy) can trigger seizures. Headaches also occur as a part of an ictal or postictal phenomenon.

**Catamenial migraine**

Increase in the frequency of migraine attacks in relation to the different phases of menstruation.

**Catamenial epilepsy**

Seizure exacerbation that occurs just before or during menstruation or at the time of ovulation.

The clinical history allows the differential diagnosis between migraine and epilepsy. During the typical migraine attack, no loss of consciousness occurs. About 20% of patients experience a visual aura. The onset is gradual, and the average duration of a migraine attack is for hours. On the other hand, the onset of epileptic attack is sudden, and an episode lasts for only minutes. An EEG is usually normal or shows nonspecific abnormalities, whereas clear-cut epileptiform abnormalities are seen in patients with epilepsy.

A migraine is a common neurological disorder, with a peak onset in adolescence, and is three times more common in women. Other family members may be suffering from the same illness. It can present with or without a visual aura. The migraine aura can precede or accompany the attack. Patients complain of visual phenomena such as dark spots, flashing lights, or blurring of vision. They can see points, lines, or stars in front of the eyes followed by a unilateral or bilateral headache. Nausea or vomiting may accompany the headache with hypersensitivity to light and sound (**photophobia** and **phonophobia**, respectively). Children may have a migraine variant called a **basilar migraine** with other visual auras, followed by spinning sensations, balance problems, nausea, or vomiting. Children with basilar migraine might rarely lose consciousness.

Some benign epilepsies, such as benign rolandic and benign occipital epilepsies, are associated with migraine. Patients with both comorbid conditions can be treated with drug choices that work for both epilepsy and prophylactic treatment of migraine. Depakote, Topamax, and Neurontin can be particularly useful in helping both problems.

**Photophobia**

An abnormal or irrational fear of light.

**Phonophobia**

Fear of sounds and noise.

**Basilar migraine**

A migraine associated with complicated symptoms such as double vision, slurred speech, loss of balance, or a brief loss of consciousness.

## 25. I am here for a second opinion. My last neurologist did not help. Every time I had a seizure, he would increase my medicine, and I experienced side effects. What can be done to control my seizures?

Choosing the right drug to control the seizures can be very challenging. This decision has to be individualized, and the benefits should outweigh the potential risks. Be sure to have open lines of communication with your doctor, asking him or her to highlight the adverse effects and safety profile of medications. The patient is started on a single antiepileptic drug and is pushed to the maximum, as tolerated. The side effects and tolerance issues may limit the escalation of the doses. If the first drug does not work, the second or third drug may work. Approximately 47% of patients are seizure free with the first drug; with the addition of a second drug, another 13% can be made seizure free. With the addition of the third drug, only 4% can be made seizure free. About 20% to 30% of patients continue to have seizures despite any combination of drugs. It is impossible to predict which drug will be the most effective for one particular patient. Some patients are hypersensitive to medications and should be tried on suboptimal doses to avoid side effects. Certain antiepileptics work well for certain epilepsy syndromes. For example, **adrenocorticotrophic hormone** works very well for **infantile spasms,** and Sabril works well in children with spasms that are associated with tuberous sclerosis. A fair trial of these medications should be given before declaring the seizures medically refractory. The patient and the family members should have a positive attitude toward epilepsy. The seizures

**Adrenocorticotrophic hormone**

This hormone is secreted from the pituitary gland and stimulates secretion of cortisol.

**Infantile spasms**

Clusters of rapid jerks followed by stiffening or jack-knife movements.

are random and unpredictable. The most common causes of breakthrough seizures (Table 15) are missing medications, sleep deprivation, physical and mental stress, alcohol provocation, or a febrile illness that is caused by an infection. For women, menstrual periods may be the triggering factor. Be sure to maintain a seizure diary. This should document the date and time of the seizure, a brief description of the seizure, any relationship to missing doses, or any other provoking factors. This useful piece of information should be shared with your physician at the next office visit.

More than 90% of epilepsy patients who go into remission do so within the first 3 years. Frequent seizures encountered during the first few months after the onset carry a poor prognosis. Patients with neurodevelopmental problems, psychiatric comorbidity, or a family history of seizures are also at a high risk of recurrence. The patients with poorly controlled seizures should have a thorough evaluation to understand their seizure type. Epilepsy surgery should be offered earlier to the patients with medically refractory seizures.

## 26. What is status epilepticus? How is it treated?

Status epilepticus is a state in which seizures occur in rapid succession without recovery to baseline in

**Table 15  Common Causes of Breakthrough Seizures**

- Sleep deprivation
- Missed medications
- Stress—physical or emotional
- Fever, infections
- Alcohol or drug withdrawal
- Menstrual cycle (for females)

between the seizures. The old definition of status was prolonged recurrent seizures lasting more than 30 minutes. The recent definitions of status epilepticus are continuous seizure activity (Figure 14) for more than 5 minutes or two or more discrete seizures between which the patient does not return to a baseline level of consciousness. The duration of seizures has been reduced, as most of the seizures tend to stop on their own in 2 to 3 minutes. Status is one of the neurologic emergencies. Status epilepticus can be convulsive or noncompulsive status. Convulsive status is easy to recognize. Nonconvulsive status may present with confused state or altered mental state without any overt convulsions, but on the EEG patients have continuous electrical activity. This activity may be confined to one hemisphere or may involve both hemispheres. Simple partial status is characterized by **focal seizures** with no alteration in the level of consciousness. One good example is simple partial seizures (motor, sensory, or psychic) as a result of brain tumor

**Focal seizures**

Older term for partial seizures; seizures coming from one discrete focus or part of the brain.

**Epilepsia partialis continua**

Continuous seizure activity in the brain originating from one side of the brain. Patients may be completely aware of the surroundings. This condition is commonly seen in patients with brain tumors.

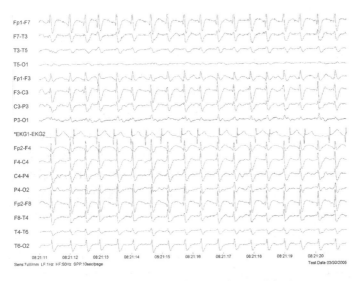

**Figure 14    EEG tracings showing continuous seizure activity (status epilepticus).**

called **epilepsia partialis continua**. Status epilepticus can occur at all ages. Over 50% of status epilepticus in children occurs in those less than 3 years old; a second peak occurs in patients over 60 years old. The highest incidence of status epilepticus is in infants, and the recurrence rate is approximately 11% in infants. In adults, the incidence is 18 of 100,000. About 126,000 to 195,000 status epilepticus events occur per year in the United States, and 22,000 to 42,000 deaths occur per year (DeLorenzo RJ, Hauser WA, Towne AR. A prospective population-based epidemiologic study of status epilepticus in Richmond, Virginia. *Neurology* 1996; 46[4]: 1029–1035). About 30% of those who present with status epilepticus develop residual epilepsy. Increased morbidity and mortality are associated with status. In children, fever, central nervous system infections, remote brain insult, or febrile seizures can present with status. Patients presenting with status epilepticus with febrile seizures have an increased likelihood of developing residual epilepsy. Mortality ranges from 3% to 4% in the pediatric population.

*Anoxia*
Lack of oxygen.

In adults, stroke, **anoxia**, low antiepileptic drug levels, and infections can result in status epilepticus, but mortality is higher, about 26%. The outcome is worse in older persons. Mortality increases with age and reaches up to 50% at the age of more than 80 years. Prehospital treatment with benzodiazepines intravenously improves outcome and reduces morbidity. The outpatient treatments available are rectal diazepam gel (Diastat, approximately 0.2 mg/kg) or intranasal or buccal midazolam (approximately 10 mg). The inpatient therapy is lorazepam (2 mg every 5 to 10 minutes, maximum 10 mg) and phenytoin and fosphenytoin (20 mg/kg). Fosphenytoin is a phosphorylated form of phenytoin. Fosphenytoin is freely soluble in solutions, can be infused faster, and causes less irritation at the site of administration compared with Dilantin. Phenobarbital can also be used intravenously at 20 mg/kg to break status. Children respond well and tolerate higher levels of phenobarbital in their blood. Most cases of status epilepticus respond to this traditional first-line emergency therapy. If this conventional therapy fails, intravenous valproic acid (Depacon) and newer drugs such as Topamax can be given through a nasogastric tube. Medications such as midazolam, barbiturates, and propofol are used to produce a medication-induced coma for 12 to 24 hours for resistant cases of status epilepticus. Medications are then backed down slowly. These medications cause decreased blood pressure and a decreased respiratory drive. This requires continuous EEG monitoring, assisted ventilation (intubation), and the use of drugs required to support blood pressure. Management of status epilepticus is challenging, and earlier appropriate intervention can improve the neurological outcome (Table 16).

The generalized epilepsies may present as prolonged status and may be of different kinds, depending on the seizure type. Examples are absence, myoclonic, clonic, tonic, or tonic–clonic status. Convulsive status bears the highest mortality and morbidity. Status epilepticus may be precipitated by several of the factors listed in Table 17. The neurologic sequelae of status epilepticus can be increased frequency of seizures, the recurrence of status epilepticus, an exposure to higher doses of anticonvulsants, and memory problems. Clinical and experimental data support that status epilepticus should be treated aggressively. The cessation of seizure activity alone does not predict a good outcome. Complications can be acute or chronic (Table 18) and may alter the clinical outcome as well. A combination of benzodiazepines

**Table 16    Management of Status Epilepticus**

- Airway, breathing, circulation
- Intubation to ensure adequate brain oxygenation
- Intravenous line
- Saline, thiamine (vitamin $B_1$), glucose
- Draw blood, get drug levels (if already on antiepileptics)
- Benzodiazepines
  - Lorazepam (Ativan)
  - Diazepam (Valium)
  - Midazolam (Versed)
  - Phenytoin and fosphenytoin
- Barbiturates
  - Phenobarbital
  - Pentobarbital
  - Amobarbital, thiopental
- Depacon (intravenous Depakote)
- Propofol
- Inhaled anesthetics
- Magnesium sulfate (used for pregnant seizure patients)
- Correct metabolic imbalance
- Prevent seizure recurrence
- Establish and treat the cause of status

and glutamate receptor antagonists in the future may improve the outcome significantly. The role of newer antiepileptics such as Topamax, Zonegran, or Keppra is being studied in animals in refractory status.

## 27. Can I take generic drugs, since brand name drugs and newer antiepileptics are so expensive?

**Brand names**

The names given to drugs by the companies who manufactures them.

Patients report higher side effects and breakthrough seizures with generic drugs compared with **brand names**. This may require more emergency or office visits or frequent blood work. The only advantage of generic drug substitution is that the patient saves money. Generic phenytoin (Phenytek) and Dilantin are

**Table 17    Causes of Status Epilepticus**

- Antiepileptic withdrawal
- Noncompliance
- Infections (meningitis or encephalitis)
- Alcohol or drug dependence
- Toxins
- Drug interactions
- Hemorrhage
- Hypoglycemia
- Electrolyte imbalance
- Trauma
- Hormonal changes
- Fever
- Sleep deprivation
- Cardiac arrhythmias
- Pseudostatus (associated with pseudoseizures); physiologic changes in status epilepticus

not clinically equivalent. Some long-acting preparations of Tegretol have no generic substitution. Physicians may dispense "brand as necessary" to ensure that brand drugs are given by the pharmacy. I usually inform my patients that potential breakthrough seizures or side effects may occur if the pharmacist gives a generic sub-

**Table 18    Complications of Status Epilepticus**

Early
- Massive release of stress hormones: risk for heart arrhythmia or cardiac arrest
- Increased heart rate, blood pressure, and blood glucose
- Respiratory failure, fluid in the lungs
- High fever and increased white blood cell counts

Late
- Blood pressure declines—30 minutes or later
- Low glucose, low oxygen, high potassium, low blood volume
- Acute renal failure as a result of lack of blood flow to the kidneys
- Aspiration pneumonia
- Diffuse swelling of the brain

stitution. The pharmacist should make sure that the color, size, and shape of the medicines are the same. Cost may be a real concern with newer antiepileptics, especially for low-income groups or uninsured patients.

Jared adds...

*The only generic I ever took was for Tegretol. I experienced no difference.*

## 28. Do I need frequent blood tests because I am taking these medications for epilepsy?

The need for blood tests varies from patient to patient. The baseline routine blood tests are advised before starting antiepileptics. Some antiepileptics can cause changes in blood tests such as a mild elevation of liver enzymes and a drop in white blood cell counts, sodium, or platelets. For example, patients on Felbatol need blood tests to monitor these blood abnormalities, every 2 weeks during the initiation phase. Patients on polytherapy compared with those on a single drug (monotherapy) can have more alterations in blood levels because of drug-to-drug interactions and are at an increased risk of developing cumulative side effects of medications. These patients may require blood tests more frequently.

Antiepileptic levels are measured in the blood (this means the amount of drug in the blood at any time). Only a part of the drug enters the bloodstream. There are two portions of the drug: free and bound. The free drug crosses the blood–brain barrier and exerts its antiepileptic action on the brain. The blood test report reflecting the drug level is the measure of the total drug (free [drug available for biological action] + bound

Treatment and Its Side Effects

[fraction bound to proteins]). Under certain circumstances, such as severe liver and kidney disease, a low protein concentration in the body (low albumin), old age, and neonatal period or pregnancy, free levels are also measured. Techniques to measure the free drug level are difficult. The free drug concentration of certain drugs can also be quickly measured in the saliva. Certain drug concentrations in the saliva such as Tegretol, Dilantin, and Zarontin correlate well with the free serum concentration. Measuring drug levels in the saliva obviates the need for a needle prick; however, measurement is more subject to error and may not be feasible.

Drugs are metabolized by the liver, is absorbed by the intestine, and is excreted in the urine and stool. Physicians monitor blood levels periodically. Drug concentrations are especially useful in

- therapy with Depakote, Tegretol, and Dilantin
- compliance with therapy
- patients with renal or hepatic disease (in whom both the free and total levels are useful)
- concomitant therapy for other medical illnesses
- extremes of age—newborns, children, and older persons
- pregnancy

Based on population statistics, the **therapeutic range** (drug levels in the blood seem to be associated with a satisfactory control of seizures) of the drug is established and guides your physicians about how the drug is metabolized or what therapeutic level is able to control your seizures. It may also be important to check compliance. Antiepileptics should be taken regularly. Any side effects that are experienced should be brought to the physician's attention. Antiepileptics should not be

**Therapeutic range**

The range of drug levels within which most patients will experience significant therapeutic effects without adverse side effects.

stopped abruptly, as this may result in status epilepticus. The medicines should only be withdrawn slowly under medical supervision. Compliance (the ability of the patient to follow the doctor's instructions, such as adherence to the medication schedule and doses or lifestyle modifications) is extremely important but can be a challenge for patients with any chronic disease. Patients must be motivated enough to ensure compliance. Patients may take a lower dose because of the side effects at prescribed doses. Patients with rare seizures tend to forget their medicines, too. The really low measured drug levels raises suspicion of noncompliance. The physician should also make sure that the patient did not miss his or her medications before increasing the doses for breakthrough seizures. Sometimes patients do not refill their medications on time, run out of medications, or forget to carry their medications with them. Patients may be given an easier schedule to facilitate compliance.

It is important to understand the maxim "always treat your patient, not the drug level." If a drug fails to control the seizures despite compliance and therapeutic levels, a new medication as monotherapy or as an adjunctive therapy is indicated for better control. Use of once-daily drugs such as Depakote ER can help with compliance.

When a physician suspects side effects of medications, the drug level is ordered to find out whether the level is supratherapeutic or in the toxic range. Some patients may not be able to tolerate side effects despite low levels, whereas others may have no tolerance issues despite high drug levels. There is no need to do frequent blood tests if someone is seizure free, free of side effects, or does not exhibit any symptoms or signs of drug **toxicity**. Table 19 lists some of the common indications for monitoring drug levels.

**Toxicity**
Adverse side effects of a drug on a patient.

**Table 19    Indications for Drug Level Monitoring**

- Symptoms or signs of drug toxicity
- Not sure whether patient is taking medications
- Patients on multiple antiepileptics
- Drug interactions are suspected
- Poor response despite good dosages
- Physiologic conditions such as pregnancy and liver or kidney disease causing alterations in the drug levels

## 29. Do I have to take medicines for the rest of my life? Can I come off of these medicines?

The long-term use of antiepileptic medications has significant adverse effects and associated morbidity. The course of the disease early in treatment provides a useful guide to long-term prognosis. The childhood-onset epilepsy may be outgrown with age, such as febrile seizures or childhood absence seizures. There are some benign forms of epilepsy, such as benign rolandic epilepsy or benign occipital epilepsy that do not even warrant treatment if seizures are rare. In contrast, those with primary generalized epilepsies such as juvenile myoclonic epilepsy may do extremely well with the lower doses but may have to take antiepileptics their entire lives.

About 60% to 75% of children and adolescents who become seizure free for more than 2 to 4 years can be weaned from antiepileptics. The recurrence risk is higher in adult-onset epilepsy compared with childhood-onset epilepsy. At least half of the recurrences occur within the initial 6 months or while medications are being tapered. Patients with a normal neurological examination, a normal brain MRI, and rare seizures can be weaned successfully. Patients with a previous neurological insult, congenital malformations, stroke, a brain tumor, mental retardation, an inborn metabolic disorder, or trauma are less likely to remain seizure free after being weaned from antiepileptics; however, some benign tumors of the brain may not need antiepileptics after complete removal. Patients with multiple seizure types have a higher relapse rate. The anticonvulsants should be tapered slowly. Abrupt cessation of anti-epileptics can result in status epilepticus.

The decision of discontinuing medications after 2 years of seizure freedom has to be individualized, and the risks and benefits should be discussed with the doctor and caregivers. In women of childbearing age, this decision may be justified considering the congenital malformation risks that are associated with the antiepileptics. In adults, these decisions may be hard to take, because the recurrence of seizures has an impact on driving or employment opportunities. About 50% of patients may be fully controlled on medications for many years. Another 25% to 30% may notice a significant improvement in their seizures on medications. Medications do not cure epilepsy. They are helpful in controlling the spread of the seizures. The anticonvulsants are tried for at least 2 to 3 years. Some patients with epilepsy may enjoy remission as indicated here:

- Newly diagnosed epilepsy: 70% to 80% controlled with medical treatment
- Five years or more of seizure freedom: 70%
- Seizure free on medication for 2 to 5 years: 75% can be weaned from medications
- Mental retardation, cerebral palsy, or other **neurological conditions**: 35%

**Neurological conditions**

Medical conditions involving the nervous system.

Patients with traumatic brain injury or hemorrhage in the brain may be put on antiepileptics for a very short time only, because no evidence suggests that the long-term use of antiepileptics will prevent late development of posttraumatic epilepsy. Patients who are seizure free after epilepsy surgery can also be completely weaned from medications or may require much lower doses to control their seizures.

Jared adds...

*This is something I worry about a lot, although I am happy to say that since my surgery I am taking considerably fewer medications in smaller doses. I worry about the long-term affects of being on antiepileptic medication.*

## 30. I am worried that I am taking too many medications. I have problems with my short-term memory. Can something be done about it?

Patients with refractory seizures may have significant cognitive issues and may simply forget to take their medicines. Patients make errors in administering drugs, because they may have difficulty understanding the physician's instructions or may get confused about their doses or dosing schedule. Drug toxicity may occur because patients get confused, think they did not take their medications, and thus take a repeat dose. They get confused over their dosing schedule or mix their generic and branded formulations. Frequent medication changes or complex medication schedules should be avoided in patients with significant memory problems unless the administration of drugs is under supervision.

Written instructions by the physicians and supervision by the family or visiting home care services can be of great help. Patients can set an alarm clock and place pills near a toothbrush or on a dining table to facilitate morning and evening doses. They can always carry the medications with them to work or school. If a dose is missed, take it as soon as possible. Calendars or pill reminder boxes can also be very helpful. Some useful tips to improve memory are provided here:

- Day planner
- Hand-held palm devices (Palm Pilot)
- A tape recorder stating appointments
- Journal
- Post-it notes
- Alarms in cell phones or palm devices as reminders

## 31. I have noticed decreased libido since I started antiepileptics. Can antiepileptics do that?

Both men and women with epilepsy can experience sexual dysfunction. This is more commonly encountered in patients with partial seizures, particularly with temporal lobe epilepsy. Women with temporal lobe epilepsy have an increased incidence of **amenorrhea** (no menstruation), irregular menstrual cycles, and decreased fertility. Women and men suffering from partial seizures complain of decreased sexual arousal and sexual drive. A reduction in sexual desire is reported in one fourth to one third of women with epilepsy.

Another common complaint in females is painful intercourse because of vaginal dryness. A study of physiologic responses to erotic stimulation found a reduction

**Amenorrhea**

Absence of regular menstruation.

in vaginal blood flow in women with epilepsy compared with a control group of women without epilepsy. In men, difficulty in achieving or maintaining an erection is possible. Dysfunction in sexual arousal is usually treated with couple counseling, enhanced foreplay, and vaginal lubrication products.

The cerebral cortex and the hippocampus influence the sexual functions in a significant manner. Certain areas of the brain are crucial in supporting sexual responsiveness and sexual desire (called **libido**). These include limbic structures in the temporal lobe and frontal lobe. Seizures cause disruption to the brain regions that control sexual behavior. Social and psychological stresses of living with epilepsy also contribute to higher rates of dysfunction. An earlier age of onset and poor seizure control are associated with hyposexuality.

Hormones are important for normal sexuality. The **hypothalamus**, the **pituitary gland**, and **gonads** intricately control sexual behavior in a feedback circuit. The hypothalamus produces a hormone called **gonadotrophin-releasing hormone**. This acts on the pituitary gland to stimulate the release of other hormones that, in turn, act on the ovaries and testes to produce sex hormones, namely, **estrogen** and **progesterone** from the ovaries and **testosterone** from the testes. Antiepileptics and a disturbance of the hormones cause abnormal sexual behavior. Women and men with epilepsy notice problems with sexual arousal more than sexual desire. Antiepileptics induce hepatic metabolism of sex hormones such as estrogens, progesterone, and testosterone. There are decreased free levels of hormones causing sexual hypofunction.

**Libido**
Desire for sex.

**Hypothalamus**
A region in the brain that controls all of the glands and the autonomic nervous system.

**Pituitary gland**
The master gland of the endocrine system. It is located at the base of the brain.

**Gonads**
Sex glands—ovaries (females), testes (males).

**Gonadotrophin-releasing hormone**
A hormone secreted by the hypothalamus, which in turn provides feedback to the pituitary and gonads.

**Estrogen**
A general term for female steroid sex hormones that are secreted by the ovary and responsible for typical female sexual characteristics.

**Progesterone**
A steroid hormone produced in the ovary. It prepares and maintains the uterus for pregnancy.

**Testosterone**
A potent androgenic hormone produced chiefly by the testes; responsible for the development of male secondary sex characteristics.

*Polycystic ovarian disease*

A disease that causes an enlarged ovary with cysts on the surface.

*Erectile dysfunction*

Impairment of achieving erection.

Antiepileptic drugs may lead to **polycystic ovarian disease**, resulting in infertility, anovulation, and irregular menstrual cycles.

Patients may not be forthcoming in discussing sexual problems, because sexuality is very private but nevertheless an extremely important part of life. Treatment includes good control of seizures, a comprehensive team approach by a neurologist, gynecologist, internist, and urologist. Biofeedback, behavioral modifications, counseling, and vaginal lubricating creams and jellies (Astroglide or KY jelly) are some of the modalities that can be used. Men with **erectile dysfunction** can be helped with psychotherapy if psychological stressors are the main cause. Certain drugs can be taken orally or can be injected into the penis. The drugs can also be inserted into the urethra at the tip of the penis. The Food and Drug administration has approved Viagra (March 1998) and Levitra (August 2003) and Cialis (November 2003) for erectile dysfunction. These can be taken an hour before sexual activity and should not be taken more than once a day.

## 32. When can I resume driving?

The driving issue is often a touchy issue, and physicians may find this aspect stressful at times. Patients who lose the right to drive can be emotionally disturbed. An inability to drive causes a loss of independence or low self-esteem. Patients may lose their jobs if driving is required. It may impose social restrictions leading to anxiety and depression. All states regulate driving with epilepsy. Physicians must understand the rules that apply to their state. Each state has set its own regulations and guidelines. Some of these guidelines need to be revised. The Academy of Neurology recommends a driving restriction of no more than 3 months after a first unprovoked grand mal seizure. It does not, however, address patients with recurrent seizures, whether treated or untreated. Guidelines do not imply that a driving restriction is always required. Restrictions may vary widely from state to state. A number of states have varying durations of seizure-free intervals, unspecified to 24 months. The Department of Motor Vehicles expects applicants to disclose information about a seizure disorder. Some states, such as California, Delaware, Nevada, New Jersey, Oregon, and Pennsylvania, require the physician to report the patient. In some other states, the patient signs the form at the time of application for a new license or renewal that the patient will inform the Department of Motor Vehicles of changes in his or her health status or driving ability. If a violation occurs, then the state may file a criminal suit against the patient. The filing is as a misdemeanor if property damage occurs. It is counted as a felony if injury or death has occurred. Patients may be provided with a copy of the rules published by the medical board that advises the Department of Motor Vehicles. Patients should self-report and abide by state driving regulations.

The physician can reflect his or her opinion on whether a patient is safe to drive. The physician may be held at fault if he or she does not warn the patient not to drive. The patient's warning should be properly documented. Patients should be free of daytime seizures that cause any subtle to frank loss of consciousness. Patients with nocturnal seizures can only drive in the daytime. Patients with syncope must abstain from driving for 1 year. If a well-controlled patient has a seizure after making changes in his or her medications on his or her own, then he or she is not allowed to drive for 6 months. If the physician recommended changes in medications, however, the patient may return to driving at the discretion of the physician. The Department of Motor Vehicles grants or refutes the driving license. A few states have mandated medical reports. Some of the favorable and nonfavorable modifiers are listed in Table 20.

Jared adds...

*I drove when I was younger when my epilepsy was under control, but I haven't in about 10 years. Things are going well after surgery, and my doctor has suggested some additional tests before granting me permission to drive again. I am hopeful.*

**Table 20    Driving Safety Issues with Seizures**

Patients Relatively Safe to Drive
- Rare provoked seizures in an otherwise well-controlled patient
- Tapering of medications under physician's supervision
- Tapering of medications while long-term EEG monitoring is done
- Nonepileptic seizures (low glucose, electrolyte imbalance, acute illness, use of drugs lowering seizure threshold)
- Brief myoclonic seizures
- Exclusively simple partial seizures (no alteration in the level of consciousness—such as psychic, sensory, visceral or autonomic auras, which are well defined and are of at least a 2-year duration)
- Exclusively nighttime seizures (for more than 2 years)

Patients Relatively Unsafe to Drive
- A history of alcohol or drug abuse
- A history of noncompliance with medications or regular follow-ups
- Letters from concerned citizens
- Prior motor vehicle accidents as a result of seizures while driving

## 33. Are there any food items that I need to avoid to prevent seizures? Should I take multivitamins?

There have not been significant randomized double-blind placebo-controlled studies to prove the correlation of certain foods and worsening of seizures. Children with epilepsy, migraine headaches, attention deficit hyperactivity disorder, or recurrent abdominal pain may have certain food allergies as triggers for epilepsy.

Patients on antiepileptics should take multivitamins and folic acid supplementation on a regular basis. This is particularly important for women of reproductive age, as both antiepileptics and folic acid depletion can cause birth defects in children of women with epilepsy. The ketogenic diet or modified Atkins diet has been useful to control seizures. Vitamin deficiencies such as $B_1$ (thiamine) are common with alcoholism and malnutrition. Thiamine deficiency can cause **dementia**, coma, and seizures and weakness or paralysis of eye muscles. Vitamin $B_6$ **(pyridoxine)** deficiency has been a well-known cause of **intractable seizures.** Calcium and magnesium deficiencies are an uncommon cause of seizures. Patients with seizures and muscle spasms **(tetany)** can benefit from magnesium and calcium supplements.

The paradox is that antiepileptics can cause a deficiency of these nutrients; for example, Dilantin use can result in lower levels of thiamine in the blood and spinal fluid. Thiamine (50 mg/day) and folic acid (1 mg/day) supplementation can improve cognitive function in epileptic patients. Red blood cell magnesium levels decrease in patients with high levels of

*Treatment and Its Side Effects*

**Dementia**
Derangement of memory—a loss of previously acquired thinking skills.

**Pyridoxine**
Vitamin $B_6$.

**Intractable seizures**
Seizures that do not respond to treatment.

**Tetany**
Muscle spasms that can benefit from magnesium and calcium supplements.

Dilantin and phenobarbital in the blood. Most of the old-fashioned drugs such as Dilantin, Tegretol, or phenobarbital cause calcium and vitamin D deficiency, resulting in osteoporosis. Calcium (1,500 mg/day), vitamin D (400 international units) supplementation, and sunlight (a natural source of vitamin D formation) can reduce the risk of osteoporosis. This is particularly important for nonambulatory, institutionalized children or older patients who get minimal exposure to sunlight and have decreased bone density because of immobility and a lack of weight-bearing exercises. Depakote may cause carnitine deficiency although the clinical relevance is undetermined. Carnitine is a nutrient needed for normal brain function and metabolism.

## 34. Can antiepileptics make you depressed or anxious? Do I need to take something for these symptoms? Will antidepressants have any interactions with the antiepileptics?

Anxiety, psychoses, depression, and mood disorders are common in patients with epilepsy. Seizures as well as antiepileptics may cause emotional, behavioral, and learning problems. There is much overlapping of the neurology and psychiatry fields when it comes to epilepsy.

Panic disorder can coexist with epilepsy. Panic episodes are characterized by episodes of intense fear accompanied by various physical symptoms. These may be pain in the stomach, nausea, chest pain, dizziness, unsteadiness, and a feeling of impending faintness, palpitations, sweating, or a choking sensation. Patients may develop significant avoidant behaviors, because they feel embarrassed by their behavior during seizures in front of their coworkers or classmates. **Agoraphobia** (morbid fear of open spaces) and **obsessive-compulsive behavior** are common in patients with epilepsy. Patients may not be forthcoming in revealing their obsessions.

Patients with epilepsy have an increased incidence of depression. Patients note changes in their appetite and sleep. In some cases, it may be situation related, such as poor control of seizures or failed epilepsy surgery. People with epilepsy attempt suicide at a higher rate than the general population. Patients tend to commit suicide with the overdose of antiepileptics or barbiturates. Depression is common in the postictal phase (period after the seizure ends).

**Mood disorders** are more common in patients with epilepsy. Mood changes during or after the seizures are usually self-limited and do not require treatment. Some patients experience a feeling of elation or euphoria as a part of their aura. These feelings may last from minutes to hours before the seizures. Sometimes behavioral problems become better before the impending seizures. In contrast, behavioral problems may be really concerning when seizures are well controlled. This abnormal relationship between abnormal mental behavior and epilepsy is called **forced normalization**. The EEG recordings of these patients become normal during the psychotic episode. Aggression, agitation, and violence are uncommon during the seizure.

Some antiepileptics do have neuropsychiatric effects of their own. Phenobarbital can cause hyperactivity and

*Treatment and Its Side Effects*

**Agoraphobia**

An unexplained fear of open spaces.

**Obsessive-compulsive behavior**

An anxiety disorder characterized by recurrent persistent obsessions or compulsions.

**Mood disorder**

Disturbances of mood such as major despression, manic, or hypomania.

**Forced normalization**

A relationship between seizure control and psychotic symptoms that exist in some patients with intractable epilepsies.

irritability in 30% to 40% of children. Dilantin can impair memory and cognition. Felbatol can worsen hypomanic or manic disorder because of its stimulant properties. Lamictal can induce or worsen underlying anxiety at higher doses.

Psychosis occurs in 2% to 7% of patients with chronic epilepsy. Postictal psychosis is seen after a seizure or a cluster of seizures. This condition includes anxiety, depressed mood, or hypomania. The psychiatric symptoms appear after a week of lucidity after a seizure(s). It can last days, but rarely weeks. Antipsychotic medications are not recommended prophylactically. Postictal psychosis is an uncommon complication of epilepsy; it is more common with temporal lobe seizures. Hypomania and mania could be part of postictal psychoses with or without hallucinations and **delusions**. Depression can be a result of the use of anticonvulsants. The use of antidepressants raises the concern of lowering seizure control. Some medications lower the seizure threshold more than others. These include tricyclic antidepressants. Rapid escalation of doses higher than 200 mg/day is associated with higher seizure rate. Another group of medications called **selective serotonin reuptake inhibitors (SSRIs)** carry a lower seizure risk compared with tricyclic antidepressants. The SSRIs are metabolized by the P-450 enzyme system of the liver. The same pathway is involved in the metabolism of antiepileptics as well. Patients may develop symptoms of toxicity of antiepileptics when SSRIs are added. Any new symptoms should be reported to your physician. High doses of Wellbutrin (Zyban, an antidepressant commonly used for smoking de-addiction also) at doses of more than 300 mg/day increase the risk of seizures. Effexor is relatively safe in patients with epilepsy. Tegretol, Depakote, and Lamictal are

**Delusions**
A false belief.

**Selective serotonin reuptake inhibitors (SSRIs)**
Medications used to treat depression, anxiety, or other psychiatric conditions. These slow down the ability of nerve cells to absorb serotonin.

good mood stabilizers and can be used in patients with epilepsy and bipolar disorders. Depakote, Tegretol, and lithium are used for acute mania. Tegretol is also found to be useful for impulsivity. Neurontin, along with other psychotropics, is used for anxiety disorder. Behavioral, supportive, and cognitive therapies, along with psychopharmacologic therapy, are useful. Relaxation techniques, yoga, and biofeedback can also prove beneficial.

## 35. I do not like to take medicines. What do you think about the alternative therapies for epilepsy treatment?

Many patients reciprocate your feelings. The dissatisfaction with the side effects of antiepileptics or poor seizure control may be some of the reasons to explore alternative therapies. There are no randomized controlled trials to prove their efficacy to date. A variety of alternative therapies, such as neurofeedback, homeopathy, acupuncture, complementary or herbal remedies, or yoga, are available (Table 21).

Neurofeedback is a form of biofeedback that may help decrease the frequency of seizures. It is an alternative,

**Table 21    Alternative Therapies**

| | |
|---|---|
| • Acupuncture | • Massage |
| • Aromatherapy | • Meditation |
| • Biofeedback | • Nutritional |
| • Chiropractic | • Osteopathy |
| • Herbal medicines | • Psychotherapy |
| • Homeopathy | • Yoga |
| • Hypnosis | |

Treatment and Its Side Effects

nonmedical, nonsurgical, noninvasive approach to treat epilepsy. The EEG activity is monitored and altered. Patients are trained to alter the frequencies of the brain waves through auditory and visual feedback. Patients receive positive feedback for the entrainment or containment of specific EEG frequency. The entrainment of 12- to 16-Hz sensorimotor rhythm is believed to decrease the seizure frequency.

Yoga is another form of alternative therapy that is used in treating people with epilepsy. Yoga is an ancient Indian practice, dating back to 2500 BCE, possibly even earlier. It is a scientific system that is designed to bring the practitioners health, happiness, and a greater sense of self. In yoga, the body and mind are linked to create a state of internal peacefulness and integration, bringing the individual from a state of separation to a self-unity that is flexible, accepting, and whole. At the practical level, and included in the contemporary definitions of yoga, are the actual physiologic/mental techniques themselves. These techniques concentrate on posture and alignment, as well as on creating a higher consciousness. Yoga uses stretching postures, breathing, and meditation techniques to calm the emotional state and the mind and to tone the body, thus decreasing the frequency of seizures. The efficacy of yoga lacks any scientific-based evidence but is a good way of relaxation and self-modulation of energy. It reduces stress and anxiety and keeps good balance between the physical and psychic body.

**Acupuncture**, a Chinese tradition, is based on the principle that specific areas of the body are charted as meridians of "energy flow." Stimulation of these specific points by fine needles balances the energy forces and can be beneficial in epilepsy and several other

*Acupuncture*

A Chinese tradition where fine needles are used to stimulate specific areas along certain meridians that balance the energy flow in that area.

medical illnesses. Needles are used to stimulate areas that are supposed to have neural connections with specific organs and body functions.

**Homeopathy** is based on the hypothesis that disease can be treated with diluted doses of various substances. Aura is believed to start from the solar plexus, and certain phases of the moon seem to precipitate the attacks, which are brought on by an overstream of mind or emotions. Bell, Bufo, Calc, Caust, Cic, Cupr, Hyos, Nux-V, or Sulph are some of the homeopathic medicines that are used to treat seizures.

**Homeopathy**

Based on the belief that a disease can be treated with diluted doses of various substances.

Certain **complementary and alternative medicines** have been used in the treatment of epilepsy, including kava, skullcap, mistletoe, and melatonin. On the other hand, St. John's wort and echinacea are commonly used herbal medicines that promote seizures.

**Complementary and alternative medicines**

This is a group of diverse medical and healthcare systems, practices, and products that are not presently considered to be part of conventional medicine.

## 36. What are the consequences of seizures?

Epilepsy, after stroke and dementia, is the third most common neurological disease. It is underrecognized in its severity, morbidity, or mortality. Sir Williams Gowers, who coined the phrase "seizures beget seizures" as a result of **kindling**, famously noted the phenomenon of epilepsy progression. The precise mechanism of seizure progression is not yet understood. It is believed that there is something called **temporal binding**, which reflects how the brain is performing important functions such as learning and memory. The brain has a local temporary network system that allows these functions. It is hypothesized that at the onset of initial injury, an alteration of temporal binding occurs. A

**Kindling**

A procedure used in animals in which unprovoked seizures can be produced by a series of provoked seizures.

**Temporal binding**

Local network systems in the brain that play an important role in cognition and perception.

group of neurons gets reorganized, and this abnormal network is somehow much more excitable or epileptogenic. Repeated seizures further strengthen these abnormal circuits in the brain by remodeling, causing repeated seizures. It is important to understand that progression of seizures does not affect all people with epilepsy. Epilepsy becomes a burden for those who continue to have seizures despite compliance.

The patient's and family's perception of quality-of-life issues is critical to understand the true burden of epilepsy. Seizures cause a significant psychosocial impact on the quality of life of patients. Seizure control is important from a medical point of view. Patients with newly diagnosed epilepsy find it hard to accept the diagnosis. Depression and anxiety are more common in patients with epilepsy who are not well controlled.

Children with epilepsy may have comorbid behavioral issues such as attention deficit hyperactivity disorder or learning disabilities. Poor seizure control can disrupt their daily activities.

**Sudden unexpected death in epilepsy**
This is sudden unexpected death in someone with epilepsy, but who was otherwise healthy and for whom no other cause of death can be found.

The death rate in people with epilepsy is twice as common as the general population. This could be as a result of life-threatening accidental or nonaccidental injuries. Some of these deaths have no apparent cause. This is called **sudden unexpected death in epilepsy**, which is 24 times more common in patients with epilepsy. This is a major concern to physicians. Most of these deaths occur during sleep and affect adults between the ages of 20 and 40 years. The risk is higher in patients with grand mal seizures. Poor compliance with treatment and low drug levels predispose to a higher risk of sudden unexpected death in epilepsy.

The possible mechanisms for sudden unexpected death in epilepsy include an irregular heartbeat, suffocation, aspiration, or fluid accumulation in the lung during the seizure. Certain factors are linked with the higher risk of sudden unexpected death in epilepsy:

1. A grand mal seizure
2. Developmental delay
3. Mental retardation
4. Missing medications
5. Several different antiepileptics
6. A frequent change in the type or dose of medication
7. Male gender

Safety becomes a concern in patients with a complex partial seizure or a grand mal seizure and in children, adolescents, or young adults who are active or may be driving. Females who are pregnant can get hurt during the seizure that can jeopardize the pregnancy. Major physical injuries such as tongue biting, a loss of teeth during falls, shoulder dislocation, hip or other long bone fractures, head trauma, body lacerations, burn injuries, and motor vehicle accidents can occur during grand mal or complex partial seizures.

Changes in mood or behavior can occur during, after, or between the seizures. Depression is at least 30% to 50% more common in patients with persistent seizures or history of a previous psychiatric diagnosis. Suicide is common and accounts for 12% of deaths in people with epilepsy. Cognitive decline is frequently encountered in patients with poorly controlled seizures or may result from polytherapy and adverse effects of medications.

Treatment and Its Side Effects

Unemployment averages about 25% in patients with active seizures. This could be due to academic under-achievement, memory problems, mood disorders, or an inability to drive to work. The social stigma attached to epilepsy may play a role in establishing relationships. Poor seizure control serves as a nidus for low self-esteem or self-adequacy feelings. The goal in a seizure patient is "no seizures, no adverse effects of antiepileptics, and good quality of life."

Jared adds…

*The phrase "seizures beget seizures" makes a lot of sense to me. Over time, it has always seemed like the more I had, the more frequently they came and with greater severity.*

## 37. What is neuropsychological testing?

Neuropsychological testing determines the brain's capability to carry out different functions such as attention, concentration, perception, visual and verbal memory, and language. Seizures can affect the performance of any of these areas. The performance of the left and right sides of the brain specific to memory and language is tested. Neuropsychologists who have PhD or PsyD training in psychology perform this test. It takes about 1 to 3 hours to perform the test. The test may at times have to be done in phases. If the testing shows poor performance in one particular field, that deficit could be a result of ongoing seizures. If the brain MRI or video EEG indicates one-sided focus, the neuropsychological testing or **WADA testing** may correlate abnormal functioning in the same areas of the brain. Neuropsychologists play a pivotal role in performing other presurgical evaluations such as WADA or brain mapping.

**WADA testing**
Presurgial testing, named after Dr. John Wada, who first performed the test.

The neuropsychologists give patients performance IQ scores and make recommendations for further treatment and for occupational and vocational retraining. If depression is affecting the ability to concentrate or is interfering with memory, they may recommend the use of antidepressants.

Neuropsychology testing can give valuable information in children by knowing the impact of seizures on the developing brain. The motor skills, language, and speech are carefully observed and compared with age-matched control subjects. Neuropsychological testing also sheds light on the social adaptive skills of children as well as other issues such as, inattention, hyperactivity, anxiety, and depression. The testing helps the children be placed in special schools or recommend early-intervention programs such as motor/speech therapy or cognitive rehabilitation.

# PART FIVE

# Children and Epilepsy

What are infantile spasms?

What are febrile seizures?

Can children outgrow epilepsy?

*More . . .*

## 38. What are febrile seizures? Do these need to be treated?

Febrile seizures occur in infants who are from 6 months to 4 years of age and occur in association with fever. These are the most common form of seizures during childhood. On average, about 33% of children who have had a febrile seizure have at least one recurrence. There is no central nervous system infection or defined direct cause of the seizure. A family history of febrile seizures may exist in the siblings, first cousins, parents, or offspring of individuals with febrile seizures. The risk of seizure is related to temperature elevation. Maternal smoking and drinking during pregnancy increase the risk of first febrile seizure. Febrile seizures can be of two kinds.

**Simple febrile seizures** are typically brief grand mal seizures that last a couple of minutes. Children do not appear sick and are seen playing by the time they are taken to the hospital. **Complex febrile seizures** are usually prolonged and may exhibit asymmetric shaking and tend to recur within 24 hours. There is an increased risk of developing epilepsy at a later age in patients who have complex partial seizures, neurodevelopmental abnormalities, recurrent febrile seizures, or an onset at less than 1 year of age.

Fewer than 10% of all of those with febrile seizures experience recurrent or severe attacks. The chances of developing epilepsy are less than 5%. Parents should be reassured and counseled about the benign nature of the febrile seizures. Most of the febrile seizures are self-limited and are genetically predetermined. Certain factors predispose a child to febrile seizures (Table 22). Treatment with an anticonvulsant is not warranted.

**Simple febrile seizures**

Seizures occurring in relation to a high fever; usually brief grand mal seizure without any focal features.

**Complex febrile seizures**

Seizures occurring in relation to high fever; usually prolonged and may show asymmetric involvement of the body or focal features clinically.

**Table 22   Risk Factors for Febrile Seizures**

- Family history of febrile seizures
- Complex febrile seizures
- Febrile seizures with small rise in body temperature
- Onset of febrile seizures before 1 year of age
- Epilepsy in first-degree relatives
- Developmental delays in the child

There is no evidence that prophylactic administration of anticonvulsants prevents later epilepsy.

Prophylactic treatment with antiepileptics is considered for complex febrile seizures only. Most febrile seizures do not require any long-term treatment with antiepileptics. Febrile status epilepticus should be treated as a medical emergency. Phenobarbital, Depakote, and Valium can prevent febrile seizure recurrence but are rarely used for febrile seizures.

Parents should use antipyretics (drugs that lower the fever) and tepid sponge bathing. Antibiotics may be needed for bacterial infections.

## 39. What are infantile spasms? How are these treated?

Infantile spasms are unique seizures with onset in infancy and early childhood. William West first described these in 1841. The motor spasm is a brief, symmetrical, bilateral contraction of the muscles of the trunk, neck, or limbs. The neck or body can bend forward, or arms may bend at the elbow. The neck may suddenly move backward and the arms or legs may straighten. These frequently occur soon after arousal and may be provoked by touch. These look like a startle response and tend to occur in clusters, varying from a couple to about 100. Patients may have very high-voltage, highly disorganized rhythms of the brain called **hypsarrhythmia**. During the spasms, however, there is sudden flattening of the background. Each spasm lasts just a couple of seconds to less than a minute.

*Hypsarrhythmia*

A distinctive EEG pattern associated with infantile spasms.

In about 40% of the cases, no obvious cause can be found. In the other 60%, prenatal, perinatal, and postnatal causes may be incriminated. Prematurity, brain malformations, genetic disorders (tuberous sclerosis), infections, inborn errors of metabolism, and head injury are some of the causes of spasms. Patients with spasms may have mental retardation and a high-voltage, disorganized EEG. This triad is called **West syndrome**. About 80% to 90% of the patients with spasms demonstrate some degree of developmental delay or mental retardation.

*West syndrome*

A syndrome characterized by infantile spasms, mental retardation, and specific EEG pattern (hypsarrhythmia).

Spasms are also associated with a genetic disorder called tuberous sclerosis classified as one type of the neurocutaneous disorder. Neurocutaneous syndromes exhibit complex neurological symptoms and signs and have characteristic skin manifestations. These are commonly associated with seizures. The approximate percentage associated with seizures in common neurocutaneous syndromes is listed here:

1. Tuberous sclerosis (approximately 80% to 90% of patients)
2. Neurofibromatosis (approximately 3% to 5%)
3. **Sturge-Weber syndrome** (approximately 90%)

*Sturge-Weber Syndrome*

A congenital disease present at birth, and characterized by a facial birthmark or port-wine stain (reddish-brown or pink discoloration of the face).

Tuberous sclerosis is a neurological disorder that affects multiple organ systems. Patients often have involvement of the brain, heart, kidneys, eyes, skin, and nails.

The skin condition is commonly confused with acne. Some patients exhibit abnormal outgrowths in the fingernails or toenails. A brain MRI will show numerous collections of abnormal neurons, clumped as **tubers** (potatoes), as indicated by arrows in Figure 15. A tuber is a benign tumor of the brain that involves the cerebral cortex. Abnormal collections of disorganized nerve cells give rise to seizures.

A second type of brain lesion is seen in patients with tuberous sclerosis near the fluid spaces called **ventricles**. These lesions abut the lining of the ventricles and are called **subependymal nodules**. These usually do not grow and do not need to be surgically removed.

The third type of brain lesion is called subependymal giant cell **astrocytoma**. Subependymal giant cell astrocytoma can obstruct the flow of brain fluid (a condition called obstructive **hydrocephalus**) (hydro = water, cephalus = brain), requiring the placement of a drainage catheter called a shunt.

Abnormal tissue proliferation can occur at other sites such as the heart or kidneys. An ultrasound of the kid-

**Children and Epilepsy**

**Tubers**
Abnormal disorganized large neuron cells in the cortex; seen in tuberous sclerosis.

**Ventricles**
Hollow cavities in the brain filled with cerebrospinal fluid.

**Subependymal nodules**
These are composed of calcified glia (supporting cells of the brain) and vascular elements that are found in the ventricles.

**Astrocytoma**
A type of brain tumor.

**Hydrocephalus**
An enlargement of the head caused by an abnormal buildup of cerebrospinal fluid (liquid that serves as an extra cushion to protect the brain and spine from damage) in the ventricles of the brain. As a result, a person with hydrocephalus may suffer mild to moderate mental retardation.

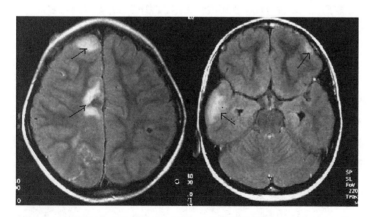

**Figure 15** MRI of the brain with multiple tubers (indicated by black arrows) in a patient with tuberous sclerosis.

neys and heart can exclude those possibilities. Mental retardation is seen in 40% to 60% of children with tuberous sclerosis. In poorly controlled patients, focal excision of the tuber causing a majority of the seizures may reduce a significant seizure burden.

**Adrenocorticotrophic hormone**

A hormone that is produced by the master pituitary gland.

Infantile spasms are treated with **adrenocorticotrophic hormone.** Because this is a steroid, long-term treatment is not desirable. Patients may demonstrate a marked improvement in their EEG pattern and reduce spasms if treated early with adrenocorticotrophic hormone. Infantile spasms associated with tuberous sclerosis respond well to an anticonvulsant called Sabril or vigabatrin. This was first marketed in the United Kingdom in 1989. The Food and Drug Administration (FDA) has not approved it because of risk of retinal toxicity. Other antiepileptics, such as Topamax, Lamictal, Depakote, or Felbatol, are also used for infantile spasms.

## 40. My child has been doing certain repetitive behaviors but is otherwise fine. I am not sure whether these are seizures.

**Benign sleep myoclonus**

A distinctive disorder of sleep in infancy characterized by rhythmic myoclonic jerks (sudden muscle contractions) that occur when the child is asleep and stop when the child is awakened.

Infants and children have intermittent recurrent behaviors that raise suspicion of epilepsy, but these paroxysmal behaviors may not be seizures. These can occur during wakefulness or sleep. For example, **benign sleep myoclonus** is common during sleep in infancy. The infants also have head banging movements while falling asleep. Some of the other sleep disorders such as nightmares, night terrors, or sleepwalking are common in children and are confused with seizures. During wakefulness, some infants show jitteriness of the whole body. Head banging, head rolling, and head rocking movements are also seen in older infants as a part of a temper tantrum. Repetitive episodes of head tilting or face deviation to one side, tics, or **tremors** are other movement disorders in children that can be mis-diagnosed as seizures. Tics can involve one or more muscle groups and can be motor or vocal or both. Facial twitching, throat clearing, grunting sounds, eye blinking, sniffling, and so forth are common tics. Abnormalities of the movements of the food pipe can cause a condition called rumination, during which the infant has protrusion of the tongue and repetitive swallowing movements soon after feeding.

Breath-holding spasms are often confused with seizures. There are two kinds of breath-holding spells: **cyanotic** and **pallid**. Fear, emotional stress, or minor injury usually precipitates cyanotic breath-holding spells. The child stops breathing abruptly, often during inspiration, turns blue or limp, and loses consciousness for 1 to 2 minutes. These begin in the second or third year of life. The second type of breath-holding spells is referred as pallid breath-holding spells. Trauma often precipitates these. The child will become limp and lose consciousness for over a minute, and parents may notice stiffening or convulsive activity because of a lack of blood supply to the brain.

Certain abnormal behaviors may be pleasurable forms of self-stimulation seen in mentally disabled children. Migraines, tremors, sleep paralysis, panic, or rage attacks are some other recurrent disorders that need to be differentiated from seizures. Video EEG is a valuable tool to differentiate these paroxysmal disorders from seizures.

*Tremors*

Involuntary trembling, usually of the hands or head; can involve the legs and the tongue or palate.

**Children and Epilepsy**

*Cyanotic*

Spells that are associated with fear, trauma, and emotional stress; child stops breathing and turns blue and may have a brief loss of consciousness.

*Pallid*

Often precipitated by trauma; child becomes limp and extremely pale with very brief loss of consciousness.

## 41. My child has speech delays. His speech therapist wants to make sure that he is not having seizures. Is this a good idea?

**Landau-Kleffner syndrome**

A rare childhood syndrome where the child has seizures and regression of language.

**Acquired epileptic aphasia**

Regression of language after normal language development; this condition is associated with seizures and behavioral problems.

**Multiple subpial transections**

This procedure is a kind of epilepsy surgery where shallow cuts are made into the brain's cerebral cortex.

Acquired speech deficits could be secondary to a rare seizure disorder called **Landau-Kleffner syndrome**, also called **acquired epileptic aphasia** (aphasia = language dysfunction). Children, more commonly boys, have a regression of language after normal language development and present with a loss of speech over days rather than weeks. Reading and writing are relatively spared. Behavioral disturbances such as rage, aggression, and hyperactivity may coexist. Seizures are rare, easy to control, and disappear by 15 years of age. An EEG will reveal more abnormalities on the left temporal region. A brain MRI will not reveal any structural abnormality. Improvement in the language is seen after epilepsy surgery **(multiple subpial transections)** in some cases.

## 42. Is it true that sometimes children can outgrow epilepsy? Can the seizures get worse?

Various benign epilepsies of infancy and childhood exist. The neonates (less than 4 weeks old) and infants (less than 1 year old) may have a seizure disorder that has a benign course. There are partial epilepsies with focal EEG abnormalities that go into spontaneous remission. Seizures end during childhood or adolescence. Children have normal developmental milestones, normal intellect, a normal brain MRI, and a normal neurological examination. No behavioral or cognitive deficits exist. Some of the benign epilepsy syndromes are briefly explained later here.

The age of onset for **benign rolandic epilepsy** is 6 to 7 years. These patients have seizures during both the daytime and nighttime. Seizures are characterized by one-sided twitching of the face or mouth. The patients may have difficulty in swallowing and are excessively drooling during the seizures. They often experience speech arrest. Grand mal seizures may rarely be present. The EEG abnormalities seem to involve the central and temporal regions of both sides of the brain. The EEG during sleep is extremely abnormal. In this disorder, the patient looks good, and recovery is the rule. EEG abnormalities linger for a few months or couple of years, even after the complete remission. Parents need to be assured that it is a benign disorder that may not even require the use of antiepileptics in 50% of patients. Antiepileptics at a low dose, are able to control grand mal seizures. Seizures go away in 99% of patients, and children may not need treatment after 13 to 16 years old.

*Benign rolandic epilepsy*

Age-related benign epilepsy syndrome, categorized as partial epilepsy; patients have nocturnal focal seizures with very abnormal EEG, normal MRI brain and neurological exams.

**Childhood epilepsy with occipital paroxysms** begins between 2 and 8 years old. The onset may be delayed until adolescence. Seizures are usually during the nighttime. Children have vomiting, deviation of the eyes, and occasional involvement of the head and the limbs. Seizures during late adolescence are characterized by visual auras and are confused with migraines. Visual auras are black and white in migraines and are usually colored in patients with occipital epilepsy. EEG abnormalities are in the occipital or back regions of the brain. The seizures remit within 1 or 2 years, and complete remission is common before the age of 12 years.

*Childhood epilepsy with occipital paroxysms*

Benign epilepsy with visual auras and EEG reveals excitation in the occipital lobes; confused with migraines.

**Childhood absence epilepsy**

Age-related benign generalized epilepsy with very brief clusters of absence seizures; also referred to as petit mal seizures.

**Juvenile absence epilepsy**

Primarily absence seizures with onset near puberty; myoclonic and grand mal seizures are also seen.

**Ohtahara's syndrome**

A neurological disorder that affects newborns, usually within the first 3 months (most often within the first 10 days) in the form of epileptic seizures.

**Doose syndrome**

A rare disorder with frequent and sudden drop attacks, violent myoclonic jerks, or abrupt loss of muscular tone (i.e., astatic seizures).

**Lennox-Gestaut syndrome**

A severe form of epilepsy that usually begins in early childhood and is characterized by frequent seizures of multiple types, mental impairment, and a particular brain wave pattern (a slow spike-and-wave pattern).

**Progressive myoclonic epilepsy**

A neurological condition characterized by myoclonic and grand mal seizures, as well as, developmental delays. It can occur during infancy.

**Childhood absence epilepsy** is one of the benign generalized epilepsies with staring spells lasting for seconds. It begins between ages 4 and 8 years. Grand mal seizures are infrequent and occur in 40% of patients. The EEG shows generalized 3-Hz spike and slow-wave discharges (typical of absence epilepsy). Some childhood absence epilepsy may go on to develop into juvenile myoclonic epilepsy. Treatment with Zarontin or Depakote controls seizures in more than 80% of the patients. Depakote is effective for both absence and grand mal seizures, whereas Zarontin is able to control absences only. The majority of the patients outgrow this disorder.

The age of onset of **juvenile absence epilepsy** is near puberty. These children have absence seizures, but the duration of absence seizures is prolonged. Grand mal seizures and myoclonic seizures are more common. Absence status can occur (continuous absence seizures for more than 30 minutes). Some patients go on to develop juvenile myoclonic epilepsy and may need treatment throughout life, but seizures may be controlled on low doses of medications. Depakote, Zarontin, and Lamictal are effective for juvenile absence epilepsy as monotherapy or in combination therapy.

In contrast, there are progressive forms of epilepsies or epilepsy syndromes during infancy, such as **Ohtahara's syndrome, Doose syndrome**, or **Lennox-Gestaut syndrome**. There is a subgroup of progressive encephalopathic epilepsies. One such example is classified as **progressive myoclonic epilepsy**, which is characterized by myoclonic and tonic–clonic seizures and progressive neurological dysfunction. The onset is delayed until late childhood or adolescence. **Ataxia** (balance problems) and dementia are commonly observed. Light, sound, and touch can precipitate the myoclonus. Some of the progressive myoclonic epilepsies are genetically determined and are transmitted through the genetic material in the **mitochondria** (fuel machinery of cells). Patients may exhibit muscle weakness (myopathy), seizures, ataxia, dementia, migraine, visual symptoms, deafness, neuropathy, or stroke-like symptoms in different forms of the mitochondrial inherited disease. The genetic testing, muscle biopsy, lactate, and pyruvate levels in the blood and cerebrospinal fluid can be helpful in diagnosing these diseases. **Neuronal ceroid lipofusci-nosis** (seizures, blindness, and mental retardation) and **Lafora disease** (partial seizures from occipital lobe, dementia, and seizures) fall under the category of progressive myoclonic epilepsy. These storage diseases can be confirmed with skin and sweat gland biopsies and genetic testing.

## 43. Does my child need to be treated after the first seizure? For how long does my child need to take medications?

The first unprovoked seizure in a child always presents a dilemma. The decision to treat should take into consideration the risk factors, the child's development, a careful history, a physical, a thorough neurological evaluation, lab data, brain MRI, and EEG. The chances of recurrent seizure after the first seizure range from 27% to 71%. Usually children are not treated with antiepileptics after the first seizure. The majority of recurrences occur within the first 6 months. Some of the predictors of recurrence in a large series of patients were as follows:

**Ataxia**

Difficulty walking or balancing.

**Mitochondria**

Cellular energy sources.

**Neuronal ceroid lipofuscinosis**

A neurodegenerative condition associated with seizures, developmental delays, and blindness.

**Lafora disease**

A form of progressive myoclonus epilepsy with psychomotor retardation, seizures (primarily myoclonic or grand mal); EEG shows occipital spikes; diagnosis made by skin biopsy and genetic testing.

*Children and Epilepsy*

*101*

1. An abnormal EEG
2. A prior febrile seizure
3. Focal weakness on one side
4. A seizure during sleep
5. A remote history of brain dysfunction

The chances of recurrence are low if the neurological exam, brain MRI, and EEG are normal. The chances of recurrence are high if children have multiple risk factors. The decision to treat has to be based on the risks and benefits of therapy compared with the risks of further seizures.

If a child has more than two seizures, the possibility of seizure recurrence is more than 80% without treatment. Children who are seizure free on medication for more than 2 years have a high probability of remaining in remission despite discontinuation. A longer seizure-free interval is associated with a lower recurrence risk; however, there is a potential risk of recurrence on withdrawal of medications. This risk has to be weighed against the risk of chronic therapy. After the antiepileptics are withdrawn, the majority of recurrences (approximately 50%) occur within the first 6 months, and more than 80% occur within 2 years. Most of the patients who relapse after discontinuation of antiepileptics regain seizure control after re-initiation of therapy. Children with a previous neurological insult, age of onset more than 12 years old, multiple seizure types, a long duration of epilepsy, and persisting EEG abnormalities have a much higher recurrence risk for seizures.

## 44. What are drop attacks? What is Lennox-Gestaut syndrome? What is the prognosis?

**Drop attacks,** also called atonic seizures, are characterized by a sudden loss of tone. These may or may not be associated with a loss of consciousness. Patients are at risk of sudden fall and associated head injuries. They usually wear a helmet to prevent head trauma. The drop attacks can be associated with tonic seizures, myoclonic, or atypical absences. All of these seizure types fall under the category of generalized epilepsy.

*Drop attacks*

A sudden loss of muscle tone resulting in falls and physical injuries. The seizures are brief, generalized and are associated with both atonic or tonic seizures.

There is a subgroup of epilepsy syndrome called Lennox-Gestaut syndrome. It manifests between 1 and 8 years old. Tonic seizures are characterized by a brief stiffening of the body that can be asymmetrical at times. These can last from seconds to less than a minute. Sometimes the seizure activity may be limited to upward deviation of the eyes and a slowing of respiration.

Atypical absences may be difficult to diagnose. Patients may stare, have eye fluttering, or have an incomplete loss of consciousness. The onset may be abrupt or gradual. Abnormal and purposeless movements of the hands (automatisms) may also be observed. These can last longer than typical absences. An EEG has a unique pattern—slower frequency (1.5 to 2.0 Hz) epileptiform discharges compared with typical 3.0 to 3.5 Hz discharges of typical absences. Patients suffer from cognitive dysfunction and/or mental retardation. At times, myoclonic seizures may be present in the Lennox-Gestaut syndrome variant with less frequent and less severe mental retardation.

Lennox-Gestaut syndrome accounts for 1% to 4% of all childhood epilepsies. The prognosis is variable and is worse in patients with earlier age of onset, with multiple seizure types, and with an increased seizure frequency. Atypical absences and myoclonic seizures are relatively easy to control. Depakote, benzodiazepines, pyridoxine, Lamictal, Topamax, and Felbatol have been useful in treating Lennox-Gestaut syndrome. Vagal nerve stimulator and corpus callosotomy are surgical options for medically refractory atonic seizures.

## 45. My child has global developmental delays and epilepsy. Is there any value of an EEG or an MRI?

Epilepsy is a major concern in the learning disabled and multidisabled population. About 40% of the institutionalized patients have epilepsy. About 10% to 20% of all learning impaired patients have epilepsy irrespective of whether they are living at home or in an institution. Epilepsy has the most significant impact on cognition. These patients' average IQ level is 10 points lower than the children without epilepsy. The underlying brain dysfunction is the most common contributor to suboptimal intellect among children with epilepsy. Learning disabilities are more prevalent among children with epilepsy. Boys are more prone to learning disabilities than girls. **Symptomatic epilepsy** caused by a brain lesion increases the chance of cognitive impairment. The lower IQ is the result of a specific neurological abnormality rather than a consequence of seizures or antiepileptic drugs. Sometimes it is not possible to see structural abnormalities on the brain MRI despite the availability of state-of-the-art technology.

**Symptomatic epilepsy**

Epilepsy where the cause of the condition is known.

Brain abnormalities can have a different impact depending on their location in the brain. These vary from being very subtle to more diffuse lesions. Brain malformations can cause mental disabilities and epilepsy. Brain abnormalities can occur as a result of brain asphyxia (lack of oxygen), infections, inborn errors of metabolism, or chromosomal disorders. The link between learning impairments, cerebral palsy, and epilepsy is well established. One third of the children with cerebral palsy develop epilepsy. In the presence of learning impairment, the risk of epilepsy is increased with the severity of mental disability.

| Neurologic condition | Seizure prevalance |
| --- | --- |
| Learning impairment | 10% |
| Cerebral palsy | 10% |
| Children with cerebral palsy and mental impairment | 50% |
| Alzheimer's disease | 8.7% |

Generalized seizures are associated with a higher degree of cognitive impairment than are partial seizures. Among generalized epilepsies, absence seizures have a very good prognosis. Patients with absence seizures have comparable IQ scores to the general population, whereas patients with atypical absence or drop attacks are linked with cognitive dysfunction. Certain encephalopathic syndromes such as infantile spasms, West syndrome, or Lennox-Gestaut syndrome have lower IQ scores as well. In children with tuberous sclerosis, the lower IQs are seen with a higher number of tuber burden in the brain. Those with onset of epilepsy at a later age, better seizure control, and a shorter duration are good prognostic factors and seem to have higher IQ scores.

This special group of children does not outgrow epilepsy. In contrast, they are usually on polytherapy and need life long treatment. Many with moderate to severe impairment are frequently institutionalized after their parents or caregivers are unable to take care of them. These children may be nonverbal and may be unable to express the auras that they experience or the side effects of their medications. Their episodes may be unrecognized, poorly witnessed, or hazily described. Their behavioral spells may be misdiagnosed as seizures.

It may be challenging to do an EEG or a video EEG in these patients. Brain MRI or EEG studies may require sedation. Because of all of these diagnostic limitations, the proper treatment approach may be delayed, or the patient may be overtreated with multiple medications. Compliance to medications is poor in patients who have mild learning impairment. Medications need to be administered under supervision in patients with moderate to severe learning impairment.

A brain MRI can determine the brain malformations, whereas an EEG can differentiate partial and generalized epilepsy and can determine the frequency of abnormal electrical discharges in the brain. These diagnostic tests provide valuable information deciding the therapeutic options and help with simplifying their medication regimens. About 60% of the mentally disabled patients can be controlled with monotherapy, whereas approximately 95% may be managed with one or two antiepileptics.

## 46. Is surgery an option in children with epilepsy?

The goal of surgery is to improve the quality of life of the children. Curative and palliative surgeries can help children to achieve their developmental milestones and have a positive impact on their brain development by reducing their seizure burden. Certain seizure disorders refractory to medicines have a higher chance of cure with surgery. Surgical cases should be carefully screened, and earlier surgical intervention should be emphasized; however, cooperation for the presurgical and surgical procedures may pose challenges.

A child's brain differs from an adult's brain. There is increased plasticity of function relative to adults. Earlier intervention for intractable seizures may help the intellectual and behavioral development. The seizure reduction as a result of surgery improves the quality of life.

Mesial temporal sclerosis does not occur until late adolescence or adulthood. Focal lesions such as brain tumors, developmental lesions such as **cortical dysplasia** (disorganized nerve cells in the cortex), or tubers (in tuberous sclerosis) can be resected surgically. Patients with congenital ischemic lesions of the brain (infantile hemiplegia), porencephalic cysts (cavity as a result of previous injury of the brain that is filled with water), and Rasmussen's encephalitis (hemimeganencephaly—half of the brain is malformed and bigger), can have a significant reduction in the number of seizures by a procedure called **hemispherectomy**. A **corpus callosotomy** is performed as a palliative procedure (the goal is seizure reduction and not cure) for drop attacks and grand mal seizures. By partial or

*Children and Epilepsy*

**Cortical dysplasia**
A malformed disorganization of the cerebral cortex.

**Hemispherectomy**
Disconnects one cerebral hemisphere from the rest of the brain. It is performed only for intractable epilepsy where one side of the brain is functioning poorly.

**Corpus callosotomy**
Disconnection of corpus callosum.

complete resection of the corpus callosum, the rapid spread of the seizures is curtailed. This surgery may not have an effect on the partial seizures but can prevent spread to the other hemisphere, thereby reducing the tonic–clonic seizures. Corpus callosotomy can reduce the seizures in more than 50% of patients. It can completely eliminate the drop attacks in 70% of patients, and the remaining 30% also demonstrate significant improvement. Noteworthy improvement also exists in daily living, behavior, and cognition. IQ points may improve by 10 points postoperatively.

The vagal nerve stimulator is also approved for use in children older than 12 years of age, although it has been implanted in younger children as well. Studies have shown not only a reduction in seizure frequency but also improvement in behavior, learning skills, memory, and overall quality of life after insertion of the vagal nerve stimulator.

## 47. What is a ketogenic diet?

A ketogenic diet is an effective therapy for pediatric epilepsy. The effect of starvation on seizures has been long studied but was first introduced in 1921. In the 1930s, Johns Hopkins University studied the effect of diet in approximately 1,000 patients. After World War II, there was emergence of the antiepileptic drugs, and the practice of using this diet dwindled. Since the mid-1980s, a resurgence of the ketogenic diet has occurred.

The diet mimics the effects of starvation by providing a high-fat, low- to moderate-protein, and very low-carbohydrate diet. It basically provides enough energy for activity and growth, thus avoiding excessive weight gain. It makes the body burn fat instead of glucose for metabolic needs. The diet causes a low blood sugar concentration and increases the concentration of the ketones in the body (ketone bodies are chemicals that are produced under stress or starvation when body fat is burned). It is poorly understood how this diet works for some children or why it does not work for others. If properly administered under careful medical supervision, the diet may completely prevent seizures in one of three children. The diet has been effective in most types of seizures. Each meal has four times as much fat as protein or carbohydrate. The fat provides about 80% of the calories. Oil, heavy cream, and margarine are used as fat sources to supplement foods. More information about different food sample choices can be obtained at http://www.ketogenic.org. Going on a ketogenic diet is a hard decision and needs perseverance and commitment. During the initiation phase, nausea, vomiting, dehydration, diarrhea, and constipation may occur. Patients show a decreased blood glucose level and increased cholesterol levels. Late complications may include bone thinning, iron deficiency anemia, and kidney stones. Most complications of the diet (Table 23) are transient and can be managed successfully by following patients carefully.

**Table 23   Complications of Ketogenic Diet**

| | |
|---|---|
| • Dehydration | • Infections |
| • Vomiting | • Bone thinning |
| • Low glucose | • High uric acid |
| • High cholesterol | • Low magnesium |
| • Constipation | • Liver inflammation |
| • Kidney stones | • Vitamin deficiency |
| • Gallstones | • Mineral deficiency |

The child is made to fast for 24 hours. This sets in the cycle of burning fat for energy instead of glucose. Dietitians give proper instructions to the parents. Patients need to understand how to weigh items and make sure that the proportion of fat and other nutrients is balanced. At home, parents can check the presence of ketone bodies in the urine by dipping the paper strips in the urine (these are called urine chemstrips).

## 48. What precautions do I need to take if my child is on a ketogenic diet? Do I expect any weight changes?

Just like any other antiepileptics, the ketogenic diet also has various side effects. Patients on a ketogenic diet exhibit reduced bone mass, which can be treated with vitamin D and calcium supplementation. Kidney stones are seen rarely. Thinning of hair or loss of hair **(alopecia)** is seen as well. It is important to watch that the calorie intake is appropriate and that the child maintains good health.

**Alopecia**

Thinning or loss of hair.

A child must finish all the food in the meal plan. One can be more creative in selecting new food items for each meal while adhering to the plan. The ketogenic diet should be stopped gradually. A sudden stop of the diet and a sudden initiation of carbohydrates may aggravate seizures and precipitate status epilepticus.

## 49. Can my child carry on regular sports and recreational activities?

Generally speaking, children with epilepsy should not have physical limitations as a result of their seizures.

The choices of sports depend on the individual patient and the type and frequency of seizures. Patients who have well-controlled seizures do not have to take the same precautions as other patients.

Swimming is a relaxing exercise and should be promoted. Studies have shown that very few seizures occur in the water. These sports can be safely enjoyed by taking a few precautions. It may not be advisable to swim alone. A lifeguard should always be on duty and should know in advance about a seizure disorder. Have practice sessions to make him or her aware of the first aid for seizures and when to call 911. If you cannot find a lifeguard, then find a companion. Make sure that you do not swim in the waters deeper than the shoulder height of your companion. Swimming should be prohibited in lakes, the sea, or very cold waters. It is also not a very good idea to swim in overcrowded pools.

Sailing and wind surfing are also allowed with a companion. Scuba diving is not recommended unless the patient is seizure free and off medications for more than 5 years or has had history of seizures only during sleep.

Kayaking can pose some problems in patients with epilepsy. Buoyancy aids worn during kayaking may keep patients pressed up under the kayak or floating on one side. Open canoes carry a lower risk.

Bicycling is advised with a friend for patients with uncontrolled seizures. Helmets should be worn at all times.

Yoga is another way of keeping yourself fit without worrying about the physical injuries that are associated with the seizures. It is a great relaxation therapy and reduces stress and anxiety, which are important for seizure control.

Patients with photosensitive epilepsy should watch television in a well-lit room and avoid strobe light in the disco or video games. They should take frequent breaks from television and computer screens. Leisure reading for prolonged periods should be avoided by patients with reading epilepsy.

# PART SIX

# *Women and Epilepsy*

What is catamenial epilepsy?

Do antiepileptics lower the efficacy of oral contraceptives?

Can I get pregnant?

*More . . .*

## 50. Do female hormones affect my epilepsy?

There are hormonal effects on seizures. The two common female hormones are estrogen and progesterone. Female hormones change the excitability of the brain and alter the threshold for seizures. Estrogen is a proconvulsant (bad guy), and progesterone is an anticonvulsant (good guy). Seizures tend to cluster in relationship to menstrual periods. This is called **catamenial epilepsy.** Seizure occurrence is related to high levels of estrogens and low levels of progesterone during different stages of the menstrual cycle. The seizure exacerbation is at least twice as high as usual. About 60% of females notice this relationship between seizures and their menstrual cycles. Different patterns of seizures have been observed in women with catamenial epilepsy. Seizures may occur during ovulation or before or during menstruation. Some women have exacerbation of seizures during the entire second half of the cycle. The reasons for catamenial epilepsy could be due to an increase in the estrogen relative to progesterone, fluid and electrolyte imbalance, psychological stress, premenstrual tension, or a decrease in the levels of antiepileptics.

**Catamenial epilepsy**
Seizures that only occur before or during menstruation or at the time of ovulation.

## 51. How do I know whether my seizures have any relationship with the menstrual cycle?

Some patients notice a clear exacerbation in seizures around a certain time of their menstrual cycle. The time of ovulation can be determined by midcycle vaginal discharge or a rise in the baseline body temperature. A thorough 4-week seizure log for at least three to four cycles should be discussed with your doctor. If a pattern is established, then the patient should undergo hormonal assessment, which should be done at or around menstrual days 4 and 22. In case the patient has irregular menstrual cycles, a lack of ovulation, or related infertility issues, a thorough gynecological evaluation is mandatory. If hormonal problems are suspected, referral to an endocrinologist is recommended.

## 52. What can be done for catamenial epilepsy?

Progesterone has a protective role and inhibits excitation of the brain. Natural or synthetic progesterone can be given in different ways to improve seizures. Natural progesterone is available in lozenge and capsule forms and can be administered in doses of 100 to 200 mg three times daily. The doses are then slowly tapered and discontinued around the premenstrual period. Some synthetic progesterone is also available in intramuscular depo forms.

Conventional antiepileptics are tried first, and hormonal therapy is tried in refractory cases and in those who demonstrate typical catamenial exacerbation. Diamox is one of the agents that is frequently used for this condition. Antiepileptic drug levels can be measured during the first few days of the menstrual cycle to determine whether the levels drop. Medication doses can be accordingly increased during that phase of the cycle when the patient is vulnerable to seizures.

## 53. My periods are irregular. Are seizures the cause?

One third to one half of patients with partial epilepsy have irregular menstrual cycles. Women with epilepsy report a lack of menstruation or lengthy (greater than 35 days) or short (less than 26 days) menstrual cycles. Seizures have a significant impact on our master pituitary gland and also on the hypothalamus. These two endocrine glands have control over the production of hormones from gonads (reproductive organs—testes in males and ovaries in females). Endocrine dysfunction is more common in women with epilepsy. A lack of ovulation is seen in 30% of women with temporal lobe epilepsy. Sexual dysfunction occurs in 14% to 50% of women with epilepsy. It could also be the result of seizure medications (e.g., Depakote may cause polycystic ovarian syndrome).

Patients with polycystic ovarian syndrome have irregular menstrual cycles or a lack of menstruation with lactation and masculinizing features (an increase in body hair, thinning of scalp hair, and acne) because of raised levels of male hormones. Their ovaries show several cysts. Patients report weight gain and decreased sexual desire. This condition is more common in women with epilepsy irrespective of what antiepileptics they are on compared with the general population.

Hormonal disturbances may be indicated if the menstrual cycle varies by more than 5 days and cycles are shorter than 23 days or longer than 35 days.

## 54. Do oral contraceptives increase the risk of seizures?

No. A common misconception is that women with epilepsy cannot use oral contraceptive pills. The studies have not demonstrated any worsening of seizures with the use of oral contraceptives. The old traditional antiepileptics such as Dilantin, phenobarbital, Mysoline, or Tegretol and newer class such as Topamax, interact with oral contraceptive pills and lower their efficacy. These drugs speed up the metabolism of the oral contraceptives. Other drugs such as Depakote, Neurontin, or Sabril do not interact with the birth control pills and thereby do not lower their efficacy. Lamictal doesn't interact with oral contraceptives, but oral contraceptives interact with Lamictal.

## 55. What oral contraceptives do you recommend?

Women with epilepsy on older antiepileptics should take higher doses of estrogen. At least 50 μg of estrogen may be required, especially if one has breakthrough bleeding. We recommend using nonhormonal methods such as an intrauterine contraceptive device or barrier methods such as condoms/sheaths, cervical diaphragm or cervical cap, and spermicides. If you are on antiepileptics such as Depakote, Lamictal, Zonegran, or Keppra, which do not interact with oral contraceptives, a normal-dose oral contraceptive pill can be used without losing efficacy. Oral contraceptives do interact with Lamictal, however. Some women prefer taking an intramuscular injection once every 3 months (a long-acting progesterone preparation in injectable form—Depo-Provera).

No studies exist that evaluate the effectiveness of Depo-Provera in women with epilepsy. Norplant, a subcutaneous slow-release progesterone preparation, is another contraceptive that protects against pregnancy for almost 3 years.

## 56. Can I get pregnant and have a healthy baby?

About 2.3 million people have epilepsy in the United States alone. Of these, 1.1 million are women. There are about 20,000 new pregnancies per year. Women with epilepsy can have normal, healthy babies. Discuss this issue with your doctor before planning pregnancy. Women with epilepsy in the reproductive age group (15 to 44 years old) should seek preconceptual counseling before planning pregnancy. The diagnosis of epilepsy should be revisited before planning pregnancy. Accurate seizure diagnosis and the correct classification of epilepsy help in picking the right therapeutic options. You might need to change drugs or their doses in order to avoid congenital malformations in the baby. Patients are asked to take folic acid supplementation for at least 1 month before conception to avoid possible malformations in the baby. I advise all of my young patients to take folic acid on a regular basis in view of the possibility of unplanned pregnancies. The dose may vary from 1 to 4 mg a day.

Pregnancy with epilepsy is considered a high-risk pregnancy. Maternal and fetal complications, such as an increased incidence of anemia, stillbirths, and prematurity in newborns, exist. The infants tend to be of low birth weight and have low Apgar scores. There is increased perinatal mortality compared with controls. Neonates may have a life-threatening disease called **hemorrhagic disease of the newborn** that occurs within the first day of life. This is characterized by internal bleeding in different organs, including the brain. Bleeding results from decreased levels of vitamin K. Antiepileptics interfere with the vitamin K transport across the placenta. Giving vitamin K supple-

**Hemorrhagic disease of the newborn**

Bleeding in the internal organs of a newborn during the first few days of life. It results from low vitamin K levels, which is an essential factor for blood clotting.

ments during the last month of pregnancy can prevent this disease. As a physician, it is my obligation to let my patients be aware of potential problems, but at the same time, I conclude my discussion with an encouraging note. Despite all of the potential risks and complications, 90% of women with epilepsy have a successful pregnancy and a healthy newborn.

## 57. What do I need to do after I get pregnant?

You should inform your neurologist or epileptologist about the pregnancy. You need closer supervision from your neurologist. A high-risk pregnancy obstetrician is preferred for prenatal checkups. Sometimes increased seizure frequency occurs during pregnancy. During the first 3 months, there may be excessive nausea or vomiting, thus compromising oral intake and the absorption of antiepileptics. Sometimes women are reluctant to take their medications, or they intentionally reduce their doses during pregnancy to avoid the adverse effects of medications on the fetus. A grand mal seizure can jeopardize the mother and the fetus. A mother can suffer from head trauma or other physical injuries. The seizure may increase the risk of congenital malformation during the first 3 months of pregnancy. Antiepileptics can increase the risk of birth defects. An ultrasound can be obtained at 16 to 19 weeks and is repeated at 22 to 24 weeks to detect possible birth defects with the use of anticonvulsants.

Folic acid requirements are increased during pregnancy. Supplementation with folic acid also prevents congenital malformations caused by antiepileptics. Pregnant mothers should try to get enough sleep and be compliant in taking medications.

## 58. Will I be on the same medications and the same doses during pregnancy?

Pregnancy is not the right time to try new medications, because it is hard to predict the response to a new drug or the risk of breakthrough seizures. The antiepileptic drug levels also decline during pregnancy because of increased blood and plasma volumes—the dilution effect. There is increased clearance by the liver and kidneys during pregnancy, causing low drug levels. Despite lower drug levels, only one third of women experience worsening of seizures. If patients are seizure free in the first 3 months, the doses are kept at a minimum to avoid the **teratogenic** side effects. The peak decline in the levels of Dilantin and phenobarbital occurs in the first trimester, whereas the decline in Tegretol levels reaches its maximum in the last 3 months of pregnancy. There are increased blood and plasma volumes along with increased metabolism of the drugs. The blood drug levels need to be monitored every month. Free drug levels should be obtained. The guidelines about using antiepileptics during pregnancy are listed in Table 24.

*Teratogenic*

Substances or agents that can interfere with normal embryonic development.

## 59. Will my seizures get worse during pregnancy?

One third of the patients may report worsening seizures. During pregnancy, changes in hormone levels occur. The worsening may be related to a relative increase in estrogen to progesterone. If the patient has been seizure free for 6 months, she seems to do well during the pregnancy, too. If a previous pregnancy had worsening of seizures, the same pattern may be

**Table 24    Guidelines for the Use of Antiepileptic Drugs During Pregnancy**

- Use the most effective antiepileptic drug at the lowest possible dose.
- Resist changing to new medications during pregnancy.
- Avoid Tegretol and Depakote, especially if there is a previous history of neural tube defect.
- Monitor the free levels of the antiepileptic drugs at each trimester, before delivery, and 6 weeks after delivery.
- Adjust the antiepileptic drug dose according to the nonprotein-bound (free) level.
- Folate supplementation at a dose of 1 to 4 mg per day before conception and throughout gestation.
- Perform an anatomical ultrasound and a maternal serum alpha-fetoprotein at 15 to 20 weeks of gestation to detect neural tube defects.
- Provide the pregnant woman with vitamin K, 10 mg per day, during the last month of gestation.

repeated. The worsening may be related to noncompliance, poor absorption of drugs because of nausea and vomiting, or a drop in the levels of antiepileptics. Women with epilepsy have an increased incidence of **preeclampsia** (increased blood pressure, losing proteins in the urine, swelling of feet). Patients with this condition can have increased seizures near the end of pregnancy or at the time of labor.

**Preeclampsia**

A condition of hypertension that occurrs during pregnancy.

## 60. Can I have a normal vaginal delivery?

There is an increased incidence of induced labor (2% to 4%) and cesarean section (two times more common than the general population) in women with epilepsy. A planned cesarean section is done in women with poorly controlled seizures. Sometimes an emergency cesarean section is done if the mother has a grand mal seizure during labor and if there is lack of cooperation on the part of mother. A cesarean section may also be chosen if the fetus shows a decreased heart rate or signs of hypoxia.

Some of the antiepileptics weaken uterine contractions. This may result in assisted delivery such as artificial rupture of membranes or induction of labor with drugs to enhance uterine contractions. The use of forcep intervention or vacuum suction to facilitate delivery is much more common in women with epilepsy.

## 61. I am taking medications for epilepsy. Will the baby have any birth defects?

The risk of congenital malformations is two times higher than in the general population. Congenital malformations can be cardiac, oral and facial, skin, nail, genital, and in the urinary tracts. Neural tube defects are commonly seen with the use of antiepileptics. These defects are characterized by the malformation of the brain, spinal cord, and their coverings. In the presence of these defects, there is increased concentration of **alpha-fetoprotein** in the mother's blood and amniotic fluid (fluid in the uterine cavity surrounding the fetus). The high alpha-fetoprotein levels in maternal blood raise suspicion of neural tube defects, which can be detected on ultrasound.

**Alpha-fetoprotein**

An antigen present in the human fetus and in diseased conditions in the adult.

**Spina bifida** is the most common neural tube defect. Patients who require higher doses of antiepileptics or who are on polytherapy (taking more than one drug) tend to have a higher incidence of neural tube defects. Depakote and Tegretol are associated with a higher incidence of neural tube defects. Folic acid supplementation at a dose of 1 mg per day helps to decrease the

**Spina bifida**

A congenital defect in the spinal column. There is an absence of vertebral arches and coverings or the whole spinal cord may be protruding outside.

incidence of teratogenicity. Women who have epilepsy and a history of neural tube defects in a prior pregnancy should take a higher dose (4 mg of folic acid per day).

In the last decade, pregnancy registries have been activated by collaborative groups of physicians in Europe (EURAP) and North America (NAREP). Australia and India recently merged into EURAP. They all enroll exposed women and monitor them prospectively with standardized methods. Even though the structure of these registries and the target populations should theoretically result in the identification of a sufficient number of women exposed to different drugs and examined for the occurrence of malformations of any type and severity, the implementation of a common database with information from the existing registries may provide valuable information in a shorter time period. Although differences between some of the registries limit the possibility to pool data, a gradual development of collaboration is highly desirable to understand the teratogenic side effects of the antiepileptics and in designing future studies.

## 62. Can I breastfeed my baby while taking medicines for epilepsy?

Breastfeeding is advocated for women with epilepsy, according to the Academy of Neurology and the American Academy of Pediatrics. The benefits of breastfeeding outweigh the potential risk of exposure of the neonate and infant to antiepileptic drugs. It is true that all antiepileptics are excreted in breast milk. Some drugs excrete in the breast milk more than others. Antiepileptic drugs cross into breast milk in an inverse proportion to their extent of protein binding. Dilantin, Gabitril, and Depakote are all extensively protein bound and have very low concentrations in breast milk. Tegretol, phenobarbital, Lamictal, Topamax, and Zonegran have low to moderate protein binding and are found to have low to moderate concentrations in breast milk in relationship to maternal concentrations. Keppra and Neurontin have no protein binding and therefore have equivalent concentrations in maternal serum and breast milk. The infant takes a longer time to clear the antiepileptic because of decreased clearance from the liver and kidney. The breastfed infant of a mother receiving antiepileptic drugs is observed for irritability, poor sleep patterns, or inadequate weight gain. For example, increased phenobarbital levels in the newborn can cause increased sedation. In that case, the breastfeeding can be intermittently supplemented with bottle feedings.

## 63. What precautions do I need to take while I am caring for my baby?

Some women with epilepsy have fears about parenting and choose not to get pregnant. Infant safety guidelines should be discussed with the patient. Taking care of a newborn is hard for anyone but may be more so for women with epilepsy, especially because sleep deprivation can cause worsening of seizures. This may require adjustments in the woman's schedule or cooperation from her spouse. The mother should try to nap with the baby to catch up on lost nighttime sleep hours. The breast milk can be expressed with the breast pump, and the partner can help with nighttime feedings. It is a good idea to keep the baby in the same room (preferably in a bassinet) as the mother.

The mother should sit on the floor or in the middle of the bed while feeding the baby to avoid the risk of dropping the baby if a seizure occurs. The baby's diaper or clothes changing should be done in a sitting position on a mat. The baby should be left in the bassinet or a crib while preparing the bottle feedings. The baby should be strapped securely if the mother opts to use a changing table. Carrying the baby in a stroller is safer than using a baby crib. When the mother is alone in the house, the baby can be given a sponge bath on the floor. A playpen can be used as a safe place for the baby.

The care of a toddler exerts more pressures on a mother with epilepsy. The house should be as child-proof as possible. The outside doors should be locked. Children should have emergency numbers to call—a friend, a neighbor, or 911. These issues need to be discussed in detail. When children grow bigger, they can be taught how to ask for help in case the mother has a seizure.

## 64. Will I stop having seizures after menopause, since my seizures are hormonally related?

Most women with epilepsy have menopause at about the same age. The usual age of onset is at 48 to 55 years (an average of 51 years). Patients with catamenial epilepsy can have menopause a decade earlier. Seizures affect the hypothalamus and pituitary, which in turn affect the gonads. Menopause causes a decline in all female hormones (such as estrogens, progesterone, and inhibin). Altered estrogens and progesterone ratios can affect the frequency of seizures. A woman with epilepsy may notice no change, improvement, or deterioration in her seizure frequency. It is more like a "wait and watch" situation. Seizure exacerbation after menopause may warrant a physician's re-evaluation or changes in medications or doses. Repeating an MRI of the brain or inpatient EEG recordings can reveal any new structural or electrophysiological changes in the brain.

Patients with catamenial epilepsy may notice worsening of seizures before and during menopause. Some women experience a reduction in seizures after menopause. Women who had an onset of seizures later in life or who have been well controlled throughout life continue to do well after menopause. The majority do not experience any change in frequency.

## 65. What is a bone densitometry (DEXA scan), and why do I need it?

Both women and men are prone to osteoporosis (thinning of bones) after the age of 40 years. Women are much more prone than men. This condition affects about 25 million Americans. During the first 5 years of menopause, the bone loss is nearly 4% to 5% per year. This bone loss is probably caused by a lack of estrogens, which are important for good bone mineralization. Other causes of this bone loss could be due to a low calcium diet, a lack of exercise, and tobacco and alcohol abuse. Women with a family history of osteoporosis are at a much higher risk. Bedridden or nursing home patients carry a higher risk of osteoporosis. Patients taking steroids, water pills, and antiepileptics have an increased incidence of osteoporosis.

Patients on antiepileptics experience bone loss at an accelerated rate. The antiepileptics stimulate the liver enzyme system that depresses formation of the active form of vitamin D, which in turn causes decreased absorption of calcium from the intestines. A DEXA scan is a test that can measure bone mineral density. It can determine your bone health and assess whether you are at a higher risk for fractures. Ideally, a baseline DEXA scan should be done at the age of 40 years. Patients on antiepileptics should have this test, especially if they have been taking first-generation antiepileptics such as Dilantin, phenobarbital, mysoline, or Tegretol for more than 5 years.

## 66. How can I prevent the natural process of bone loss?

Patients on antiepileptics should take calcium (1,500 mg/day) and vitamin D (400 international units) supplements. These are essential for healthy bone mineralization. Bone is constantly undergoing breakdown and renewal processes. Until 30 years of age, bone formation is more than the bone loss. The average daily requirements are 1,500 mg of calcium before puberty, during pregnancy, and after menopause. After puberty, this requirement is slightly less, about 1,000 mg per day, as bone formation reaches its peak at 20 years of age. Patients who are at risk of fractures are prescribed biphosphonates (e.g., Fosamax, Actonel, didronel) or parathyroid hormone analogue (Teriparatide). Estrogens are important for bone health. Hormonal therapy is recommended for osteoporosis in some postmenopausal women. General measures such as good nutrition, an active lifestyle, and regular exercising such as running, weight lifting, or brisk walking, and gravity-resisting exercises can help to decrease bone loss.

## 67. Do you recommend hormonal replacement therapy to reduce the risk of osteoporosis?

Hormonal replacement therapy is recommended for the treatment of postmenopausal symptoms. Hormonal replacement therapy reduces the risk of heart disease and osteoporosis. It can also help in controlling common postmenopausal symptoms such as hot flashes, dryness of the vagina, and insomnia. Some of the risks involved with hormonal replacement therapy are an increased risk of breast and endometrial cancer. Antiepileptics interact with the hormonal therapy, and some women may experience worsening of seizures. Natural progesterone is more beneficial in controlling seizures than synthetic progesterone. Hormonal supplementation should be given judiciously.

## 68. Will my medications change after menopause?

The medications do not necessarily need to be changed. Doses may be altered because of changes in metabolism. Drugs that are known to increase risk of osteoporosis may be changed to newer antiepileptics. Older people are prone to other medical illnesses such as heart disease, diabetes, stroke, or depression. They may be taking other medicines along with antiepileptics. Some patients may be taking Coumadin for stroke prophylaxis. Sometimes, antiepileptics with the least drug-to-drug interactions, such as Keppra or Neurontin, may be more reasonable options than older medications. The need to continue these can be reassessed if the patient has been seizure free for a long time.

# PART SEVEN

# *Epilepsy in Older People*

Will antiepileptics have interactions with
other medicines I am on now?

Can I take cough medicines or antibiotics as needed
without worrying about drug interactions?

*More . . .*

## 69. I am 68 years old and am taking prescription drugs. Do antiepileptics have any interactions with my existing drugs?

The incidence of epilepsy is highest in the older population compared with any other age group. Stroke accounts for 30% to 40% of all identifiable causes of epilepsy in older people. Brain tumor, head trauma, and neurodegenerative diseases such as Alzheimer's disease are some other causes.

Antiepileptics are frequently prescribed in nursing home patients for epilepsy or nonepilepsy conditions. Other disorders for which anticonvulsants are prescribed are neuralgias, essential tremor, restless leg syndrome, or behavioral disorders. The metabolism of the body slows down overall. The protein concentrations are low. The drugs bind to the proteins. In the presence of low concentrations of proteins, the unbound fraction of the drug increases. Age-related decreased clearance of drugs through the liver and kidneys also increases the unbound fraction of the drug. Older patients may have comorbid medical illnesses such as heart problems, diabetes, high cholesterol, memory, balance, or urinary problems. Some may have difficulty ambulating or significant visual or hearing deficits. They may be on multiple other medications and may develop drug interactions. Old traditional antiepileptics induce liver enzyme systems, and simultaneous administration of other drugs may alter the levels of the antiepileptics.

1. *Drug interactions:* Concomitant medications taken by older patients can modify the absorption, distribution, and metabolism of the antiepileptics. There is an increased risk of toxicity or therapeutic

failure. Keppra, Lamictal, and Neurontin have the least drug-to-drug interactions. These may be good choices if someone is on blood thinners such as Coumadin.

2. *Hyponatremia:* Tegretol and Trileptal can cause lower sodium, which may become significant in an older person who is taking water pills or is on a salt-restricted diet because of high blood pressure.

3. *Osteoporosis:* Phenobarbital, Dilantin, Tegretol, and Mysoline increase the risk of osteoporosis. This may be significant in patients who are bedridden or living in a nursing home and are having difficulty with ambulation or inadequate exposure to sunlight (sunlight is the natural way of synthesizing vitamin D). Females are more prone to osteoporosis than men after 40 years of age. Calcium (1,500 mg/day), vitamin D (400 international units), Fosamax, and adequate sunlight exposure can prevent the risk of osteoporotic hip or spine fractures.

4. *Cognition:* Phenobarbital, Dilantin, and Mysoline can cause significant sedation and cognitive difficulties. Older people are more prone to these problems than the general population. Topamax can worsen cognitive faculties, too. More activating drugs, such as Lamictal, may be reasonable under such conditions. Patients with memory problems can benefit from antiepileptics with easy dosing or a single-dose schedule.

5. *Cost:* Cost may be a serious issue in this age group who average more than six prescription drugs. Despite better tolerability and a better safety profile, newer antiepileptics may not be practically feasible.

**Diabetes mellitus**

Diabetes caused by a relative or absolute deficiency of insulin.

6. *Weight changes:* Weight gain may not be desirable in an older person with **diabetes mellitus**. Patients on antiepileptics such as Depakote, Neurontin, or Tegretol have to be watched carefully for any significant weight gain. Lamictal is a more weight-neutral drug and may be preferred in diabetics.

7. *Heart diseases:* Dilantin and Tegretol are old antiepileptics and should be avoided in heart patients. In nursing homes, Dilantin is most commonly used. In emergency rooms in most community and even in large hospital centers, Dilantin is infused intravenously and can cause decreased blood pressure and cardiac complications. Both Dilantin and Tegretol can cause heart block or arrhythmia of the heart. The older population is more susceptible to these side effects compared with a younger population. Fosphenytoin can decrease these cardiovascular complications and can be infused at a faster rate.

8. *Renal and hepatic diseases:* The doses of antiepileptics have to be adjusted. Certain antiepileptics have to be avoided if they are metabolized primarily by the liver or kidneys.

**Parkinson's disease**

A degenerative disorder of the central nervous system characterized by tremor and impaired muscular coordination.

**Hypothyroidism**

Insufficient production of thyroid hormone levels in the body.

9. *Movement disorders:* Depakote may worsen the symptoms of **Parkinson's disease** and thus should be avoided in these patients. Depakote is frequently associated with tremors, although any antiepileptics can cause tremors. Depakote should be avoided in patients with essential tremors. Mysoline (primidone) is a first-generation antiepileptic that is frequently used in the treatment of essential tremor.

10. *Thyroid disorders:* Most of the antiepileptics cause **hypothyroidism** (a low functional state of the thyroid gland). Patients should be watched for clini-

cal symptoms of hypothyroidism. Thyroid hormone levels in the blood should be assessed carefully in patients with thyroid disease.

11. *Psychiatric disorders:* Patients may be taking psychotropic medications for psychiatric diseases. The interaction of antiepileptics with the antipsychotic drugs is intricate.

Older patients are more sensitive to the central nervous system side effects of antiepileptics or antipsychotic drugs. This sensitivity is independent of drug concentration. Some antipsychotics may lower the seizure threshold. One such example is Wellbutrin, an antidepressant that at higher doses (> 300 mg per day) can lower the seizure threshold. Ginkgo biloba, a commonly used herb for cognitive enhancement, may also be a proconvulsant. Patients who have epilepsy and are taking antipsychotic drugs may need a higher dose of antiepileptics.

## 70. My internist wanted to know whether I can take other medications with antiepileptics. Can I take cough medicines or antibiotics as needed without worrying about drug interactions?

Patients with epilepsy may have other comorbid medical conditions. Prescriptions for other concurrent medical illness represent a dilemma for the physicians. It is very crucial to have knowledge of adverse drug reactions and drug interactions.

A drug interaction can be defined as a change in the effectiveness of a drug or symptoms and signs of toxicity when another drug or substance is added. The added drug can change drug absorption, distribution, protein binding, metabolism, penetration to the blood–brain barrier, or excretion of the drug. The addition or deletion of the antiepileptic or other drug may change the dose requirement. Cytochrome P-450 (CYP-450) is a microsomal enzyme system that is embedded in the cell membrane of the liver cells. About 30 different types of enzymes exist in this complex unit. The major type responsible for drug metabolism is CYP3A4. Drug interactions involving the CYP-450 enzyme system are the result of two different processes: inhibition and induction. Inhibition slows the metabolism and induction speeds the metabolism. Increased metabolism results in a decreased drug level, whereas decreased metabolism causes an increased drug level.

Antacids can affect drug binding and should be separated from antiepileptics by 2 hours.

Laxatives increase the motility of the stomach and intestine and thereby can affect the absorption of the antiepileptics.

Common sedatives used for sleep disorders can enhance the fundamental sedative properties of antiepileptics.

Antibiotics such as imipenem or ciprofloxacin can lower the seizure threshold. The choice of antibiotics should be on the basis of the culture and sensitivity report rather than its concern for causing seizures. The use of erythromycin in patients using Tegretol can bring out symptoms and signs of Tegretol toxicity.

Some of the HIV and other antiviral drugs can increase the seizure risk as well.

About 50% of the epilepsy patients harbor feelings of depression. The tricyclic antidepressants are metabolized faster in the presence of anticonvulsants, thereby reducing their antidepressant effects. In contrast, some tricyclic antidepressants increase the level of antiepileptics. Some antidepressants, such as clomipramine, maprotiline, or Wellbutrin at higher doses have increased inherent epileptogenic potential. The choice of antidepressants should be based on individual needs without worrying about the seizure control. Drugs such as Haldol and Clozaril have a higher propensity for seizures.

Epilepsy is frequently associated with anxiety and panic disorder. Many patients are prescribed benzodiazepines for these indications. An abrupt withdrawal from benzodiazepines can cause seizures. There is increased risk of withdrawal seizures, especially after higher doses and chronic use. Drugs such as Dilantin and Tegretol can lower benzodiazepines levels, precipitating withdrawal seizures.

Analgesics such as tramadol (Ultram), propoxyphene, Demerol, and "Ts and blues" have resulted in seizures. Patients with a history of drug abuse who are currently on methadone find difficulty using Dilantin and Tegretol. They claim that anticonvulsants "eat their methadone."

Epilepsy in Older People

Antihistamines are used in common cough and cold medicines and sleeping pills. Antihistaminics lower the seizure threshold.

Amphetamines are commonly used to treat attention deficit hyperactivity disorder in children. Amphetamines can rarely cause seizures. This risk is much higher when these are combined with an antidepressant such as Zoloft.

Enzyme inducers of CYP3A4 such as Dilantin, Tegretol, Mysoline, and phenobarbital can lower the efficacy of oral contraceptives, resulting in breakthrough bleeding or unwanted pregnancies. Other alternatives such as Depakote, Neurontin, or Lamictal have fewer interactions with oral contraceptive pills. However, oral contraceptives do interact with Lamictal.

Enzyme inducers such as phenobarbital, Tegretol, and Dilantin can induce the metabolism of Coumadin. Dilantin and Coumadin get metabolized by the CYP2C9 isoenzyme of the P-450 system. This competition for the same site can cause alterations in concentrations of Coumadin in blood. Coumadin doses may need to be adjusted accordingly. Other antiepileptics such as Keppra, Neurontin, and Lamictal may be chosen because they have fewer drug interactions with Coumadin.

Cyclosporine also gets metabolized by CYP3A4 and can change the antiepileptic drug levels.

# PART EIGHT

# *Presurgical Evaluation and Epilepsy Surgery*

What is an angiogram?

What is temporal and extratemporal lobe surgery?

What are the complications of epilepsy surgery?

*More . . .*

## 71. What is a WADA test?

WADA, an important presurgical test, is named after Dr. Juhn Wada, who first performed this test. This procedure is also called the **intracarotid sodium amobarbital procedure**. This is a standard part of temporal lobectomy evaluation. The patient undergoes a **cerebral angiogram**. A cerebral angiogram visualizes blood vessels that supply blood to the brain. The neuroradiologist inserts a catheter (a long, narrow tube) into an artery in the groin under local anesthesia. The catheter is directed to the right or left internal carotid artery in the neck, which supplies blood to the brain. Through the catheter, a dye called sodium amobarbital is injected. Most patients may feel a warm sensation while the dye is being injected. This dye flows through the blood vessels of the brain; images are then taken. After the angiogram is done, the catheter will stay in place for the WADA.

The flow of the dye is studied in the form of the radiological pictures called a cerebral angiogram (cerebral = brain; angio = vessels). The abnormal anatomy of the brain vessels can also be determined with the help of the test. The side of the brain with the seizure focus is always studied first. After an angiography of the brain, sodium amobarbital is injected into each side. Half of the brain is put to sleep transiently, just like an artificially induced transient paralysis of the brain. As the effect of the drug wears off, the brain functions are fully regained. After the injection and during the maximal drug effect, language and memory are studied individually on each side. Language is usually a left-hemisphere function. About 90% or more of right-handed patients have language function on the left side. WADA will tell the physicians which side controls language in your brain. Language is assessed by

**Intracarotid sodium amobarbital procedure**

Also called WADA test, used to localize speech and memory function prior to surgical treatment of temporal lobe seizures.

**Cerebral angiogram**

An x-ray of the arteries and veins in the brain. For the test, a contrast dye is passed into blood vessels through a catheter.

the ability to comprehend, express, repeat, and name pictures, body parts, or common objects. Memory is tested by asking the patient to repeat numbers and providing different visual clues such as common drawings, printed words, colored shapes, or simple arithmetic problems.

If the right carotid artery is injected, the right side of brain goes to sleep and cannot communicate with the left side. After just a few minutes, the sodium amobarbital wears off. The side that was asleep starts to regain its functions. After both sides of your brain are fully awake, the neuropsychologist will ask you what was shown. If you do not remember what you saw, items are shown one at a time, and you are asked whether you saw each one before. The neuropsychologist records your responses.

After a delay, the other side of the brain is put to sleep. To do this, the catheter is withdrawn part of the way and threaded into the internal carotid artery on the other side. A new angiogram is done for that side of the brain. Different objects and pictures are shown, and the side that is awake (which was asleep before) tries to recognize and remember what it sees. After both sides are awake again, you will be asked what was shown the second time. Then you are shown items one at a time and asked whether you just saw each item. The patients' language side and memory scores are charted. The aim of this test is minimize the risks of any language and memory deficits after epilepsy surgery. If the patient has poor memory on the affected side, the surgery did not affect the patient's memory. In contrast, the patient's memory can be affected significantly postoperatively if memory scores were good on the side where surgery is being performed.

## 72. Who performs the WADA test?

The WADA test needs a team approach. This includes a neuroradiologist (who does the angiogram and analyzes the images of the vessels), the epileptologist (a neurologist with specialization in treating patients with epilepsy and reading EEGs), and the neuropsychologist (a specialist who deals with performance, thinking, and behavior of the brain).

## 73. Is the WADA an outpatient test?

The WADA test is usually done as an outpatient procedure. It takes about 4 to 6 hours on average. In some centers, the delay between the injections is 30 to 60 minutes. Sometimes a patient may have a seizure on the table, thus delaying the procedure. A patient may be in a confused state after the seizure and may not be able to cooperate for the test. Rarely, patients become confused after heavy doses of amobarbital, and their performance on the test may be clouded by other factors. Some centers test one side on one day and test the other side the following day. Between 5 and 12 items are shown to each side of the brain. You may come in and leave the same day after a few hours. The site where the catheter is inserted is watched carefully for any bleeding. In case of any complications, your doctor may ask you to stay slightly longer, and you may be discharged the following day.

## 74. What are the complications of an angiogram?

The WADA test is generally safe. Like any other invasive surgical procedure, however, a slight risk of complications exists. These complications can be as minor as pain or infection at the catheter site or as serious as a potential stroke. Because the WADA involves entering the arteries, there is a chance that fat inside an artery may come loose and cause blockage of vessels in the brain, leading to a stroke. This risk of stroke is less than 1%; however, it may be slightly higher for older patients who have a known history of high cholesterol or **atherosclerosis** (cholesterol deposition in the walls of blood vessels).

**Atherosclerosis**

The progressive narrowing and hardening of the arteries.

## 75. When is epilepsy surgery considered?

Surgery is an alternative for some patients whose seizures cannot be controlled by medications. *Seizures beget seizures.* It is important to keep both small or big seizures under control. Seizures have a significant impact on the patient's life. Tonic–clonic seizures are associated with serious physical injuries or sudden unexplained death. Frequent seizures may alter educational plans or occupational opportunities. Epilepsy has a negative impact on cognition and several other quality-of-life issues. Epilepsy is medically refractory in 20% to 30% of cases. At least two single drugs and a combination of two or more drugs should be tried before surgery is considered. The chances that the third drug will cure the seizures are less than 5%. On the other hand, carefully selected temporal lobe resection can result in up to 80% to 90% seizure freedom. Patients with hippocampal atrophy and mesial temporal sclerosis on an MRI tend to do much better than extratemporal surgeries. The use of epilepsy surgery was increased in the 1980s and 1990s. Temporal lobe surgery is the most common epilepsy surgery performed. Nevertheless, brain surgery carries its own risk (Table 25).

**Table 25    Complications of Temporal Lobectomy**

- Hemorrhage
- Infection
- Stroke
- Hydrocephalus (increased cerebrospinal fluid)
- Mild visual field cut
- Third cranial nerve palsy
- Memory deficits
- Bone resorption

The benefits of surgery should be weighed carefully against its risks. In the past, patients did not consider this option despite several failed medication trials. More recently, studies have shown that surgical outcome is better with an earlier intervention. This is particularly true for children who have a developing brain, and ongoing seizures can interfere with their cognition and learning abilities. Surgery is now being performed on some patients whose seizures have been uncontrolled for only 1 or 2 years. A patient should have documented epileptic seizures, have failed at least two standard therapies, and should have seizures starting from one part of the brain and that part can be removed without affecting speech, movements, sensation, memory, or vision.

Epilepsy surgery can prove beneficial to patients who have seizures associated with structural brain abnormalities such as benign brain tumors, congenital strokes, traumatic brain injury, and malformations of blood vessels. It is not useful if the onset of the seizures is diffuse or does not involve a specific area. The few pertinent questions in your doctor's mind before considering surgery are as follows:

1. Are the seizures refractory to treatment?

2. Is there any particular area of the brain where the seizures start?

3. Is it safe to take out or alter this abnormal electrical network area?

Epilepsy surgery can be done as a single-stage, two-stage, or three-stage procedure. In some cases, the patient may be awake during part of the surgery.

## 76. How is epilepsy surgery done?

There are different kinds of epilepsy surgeries. Epilepsy surgery can be broadly categorized into two kinds:

A. Removal, **ablation**, or disconnection
   1. Temporal lobectomy
   2. Functional lobectomy
   3. Lesionectomy
   4. Corpus callosotomy
   5. Subpial transection
   6. Deep brain ablation
B. Implantation or augmentation
   1. Vagal nerve stimulation
   2. **Deep brain stimulation**
   3. Closed loop cortical stimulation

Epilepsy surgery is done most commonly in patients with temporal lobe epilepsy. There are two main types of brain surgery for epilepsy. The first, and by far the most common, is called **resection** or resective surgery. In this type, the surgeon removes the area of the brain that causes the patient's seizures. The most common example of this type of surgery is **temporal lobectomy,**

**Ablation**

A procedure that removes damaged tissues using heat sources.

**Deep brain stimulation**

A treatment where a probe or electrode is implanted and used to stimulate a clearly defined, abnormally discharging brain region to block the abnormal activity.

**Resection**

Excision of a portion or all of an organ or other structure.

**Temporal lobectomy**

A procedure to remove the part of the brain that is involved with speech, language, memory, and the perception of smell and taste.

*143*

in which part of the temporal lobe of the brain is removed; however, a similar operation can be performed on the frontal, parietal, or occipital lobe on the right or left side of brain, and seizure focus can be removed without compromising the vital functions of the brain. Sometimes, there may be more than one seizure focus requiring a larger area of resection. Complete excision of a discrete resectable epileptogenic lesion carries at least an 80% chance of favorable outcome.

**Lesionectomy**

Removal of a lesion (pathological or traumatic discontinuity of tissue).

**Lesionectomy** is removal of an abnormal area of structural deformity evident on the brain MRI as well as removal of any abnormal surrounding epileptogenic zone based on intracranial data and brain mapping. The outcome of lesionectomy is usually excellent.

**Disconnection**

Surgical resection of neuronal pathways that connect two areas of the brain.

Another kind of epilepsy surgery interrupts neuronal pathways that inhibit the seizure spread. The term **disconnection** is sometimes used to describe it. One example of this kind of procedure is called a corpus callosotomy. The corpus callosum is a thick band of nerve fibers that connects two halves of the brain. This structure helps two parts of the brain communicate with each other and integrate functions. The disconnection helps confine the seizures to one part of the brain, reducing generalized seizures or drop attacks, which carry a significant morbidity and mortality. It is also done for patients with a partial seizure onset with spread to the other hemisphere, but it is hard to localize exactly the abnormal focus; thus, resection may result in significant deficits. By doing a corpus callosotomy, the seizures remain confined to the hemisphere of origin and do not generalize. It can be carried out in either a one- or two-staged procedure. It has a desynchronizing and inhibitory effect on the seizures. It is especially performed for tonic, atonic, myoclonic, or partial seizures with frequent secondary generalization. It can also be combined with resection surgeries such as in frontal lobe seizures (frontal lobe seizures quickly spread to the other part through the corpus callosum). This is considered a palliative procedure to reduce the severity of the seizures. No one should assume that seizures will stop completely. However, it significantly reduces the risk of physical injuries associated with grand mal seizures.

A procedure called **multiple subpial transections** is another example of disconnection surgery. It involves cutting neuronal pathways. This procedure may be helpful when seizures begin in areas that are too important to remove. This may be more of a palliative procedure.

A **hemispherectomy** (hemi = half, sphere = hemisphere, ectomy = resection) removes all or almost all of the brain. It is like functioning with half of the brain. It is frequently done for Rasmussen's encephalitis in children. Rasmussen's encephalitis is an immune disorder in which a previously normal child has uncontrolled seizures involving half of the body refractory to all medical treatments. Patients exhibit progressive atrophy (shrinkage of the half of the brain on an MRI) and weakness of one entire side of the body. Hemispherectomies are also done in patients with a massive congenital stroke or bleeding causing extensive damage to almost one entire side of the brain. It makes sense to do this surgery in cases in which one side has already lost its function because of massive damage to that area but the damaged tissue is extremely excitable causing frequent multiple seizures. Table 26 lists some of the indications for which hemispherectomies are performed. The expectations should be clearly discussed with the family beforehand. Worsening of the

**Multiple subpial transections**

This procedure is a kind of epilepsy surgery where small shallow cuts are made into the brain's cerebral cortex.

**Hemispherectomy**

To remove all or almost all of the brain.

**Presurgical Evaluation and Epilepsy Surgery**

**Table 26    Indications of Hemispherectomy**

- Rasmussen's encephalitis
- Traumatic brain injury
- Congenital stroke
- Viral or bacterial infection
- Migrational disorders of the brain
- Sturge-Weber syndrome

motor or sensory deficits may occur after the hemispherectomy. This weakness may improve after a month. Patients may be able to walk or use their arm, but toe tapping or finger movements may not return.

## 77. What is brain mapping?

Different regions in the brain have specific functions. It is important to understand the functions of the areas affected by seizures. Surgery is planned in such a way that all vital functions such as movements, sensations, vision, hearing, and language remain undisturbed. Brain mapping identifies these regions. We have a good understanding of these areas and their roles and locations. The brain has a lot of plasticity. Because of the impact of the seizures and different pathologies, such as stroke, tumor, trauma, or blood vessel abnormality, some overlapping regions may be trying to compensate for the diseased or nonfunctional area. Therefore, neurosurgeons and epileptologists need to identify these locations and their functions precisely.

During electrical brain mapping, the brain is stimulated to determine the specific function of a particular area. A very low current is applied to a very small area of the brain's surface, thus interfering with how the area normally works. After the current stops, that part of the brain resumes its usual activity. Gradually, the current is increased until a preset maximum is reached or until a significant response is seen. Then a new location in that region is chosen, and the physician starts over with the lowest current. Each location is tested in this way to create an accurate "map" of functions present within that region of the patient's brain. The epileptologist provides to the neurosurgeon a map showing the following regions in the brain:

1. Seizure focus
2. Predominant epileptiform discharges (epilepsy brain waves)
3. Specific functional areas of the brain showing motor, sensory, and language areas of the brain

This demarcation helps neurosurgeons tailor the surgical resection. An attempt is made to resect completely the seizure focus and surrounding abnormal epileptogenic tissue without compromising the vital functional areas. Brain mapping can also be performed while the brain surgery is being performed.

## 78. How long does brain mapping take?

The length of the mapping procedure depends on how much brain tissue is targeted for surgery, how many locations need to be tested, and what kind of function is expected in those areas. Mapping may last anywhere from one to several hours. The total duration also depends on the patient's cooperation. Seizure during the mapping either spontaneously or as a result of stimulation can also delay the procedure. Patients may not be able to cooperate because of periods of confusion after the seizure. If a patient does have a seizure, mapping is temporarily stopped until the patient has fully recovered to his or her baseline.

## 79. What are the risks of electrical brain mapping?

Brain mapping has a few risks. The main risk is that a seizure may be triggered. The areas being mapped are usually close to where the patient's seizures ordinarily begin. Electrical stimulation of the electrodes can initiate epileptiform discharges or patients' typical seizures. The stimulation can be immediately stopped as soon as epileptiform discharges are seen to build up or the patient goes into a seizure. Some of these discharges can be stopped abruptly by giving an additional brief pulse of current to the same area. If the area being mapped is very irritable, the patient is often given a powerful anti-seizure medication before receiving any further electrical stimulation. There is a relatively small risk of pain during electrical stimulation. Even though the brain itself does not sense the currents, an electrode occasionally makes contact with the membranes surrounding the brain. Patient may feel a tingling sensation when the current is applied. Because the physician always starts at a low current, these contacts are easily identified, and stimulation with higher currents is avoided to decrease discomfort.

## 80. How is the brain mapped during surgery?

Electrical brain mapping can also be performed during any surgery that exposes part of the brain. This is called intraoperative brain mapping because it occurs during an operation. Using a small electrical probe, the surgeon tests the locations on the brain's surface one after another to create a map of functions. Any number of locations can be tested. The motor function can be assessed intraoperatively even under sedation. To map other functions such as language, sensation, or vision, the patient must be awake to participate. Intraoperative mapping is often done when previous extraoperative mapping found important functions very close to the area targeted for surgery.

## 81. What functions are mapped electrically?

Usually language, motor, sensory, and visual functions are mapped. During language testing, different aspects of language such as comprehension, expression, repetition, and naming are checked individually (see Figure 16a). During the stimulation, negative (weakness or numbness of the face, arm, or leg and facial droop) or positive (jaw protrusion, twitching or tingling, painful or electrical feeling involving face, arm, or leg) motor or sensory function is carefully noted. This information is depicted in the brain maps to help the neurosurgeon recognize important functional areas of the brain. The stimulation of the speech center may result in problems with comprehension, expression, naming, or repetition.

## 82. What do you mean by one-stage, two-stage, or three-stage epilepsy surgery?

As the name suggests, this epilepsy surgery can be done as a one-stage, two-stage, or three-stage procedure. One-stage surgery refers to craniotomy (removal of the skull bone), exposure of the surface of the brain, and removal of the abnormal epileptogenic area. This is done for cases in which presurgical data indicate a clear-cut focal area of seizure onset. EEG, video EEG, and brain MRI or other neuroimaging and WADA tests have indicated a single-seizure focus.

A two-stage surgery involves two sets of brain surgeries. During the first stage, a surgeon creates an opening in the skull and exposes the surface of the brain. No brain tissue is removed, but small electrical contacts, or electrodes, are placed over the surface of the brain. These electrodes can be small rectangular strips or a 64-contact grid. After these electrodes are in place, the scalp is closed. The patient then returns to a hospital bed and is closely monitored. The EEG recording done in this manner is called "intracranial EEG monitoring." The electrodes record the patient's seizures electrically, and the epileptologist draws a map for the neurosurgeon (Figure 16b). It also allows brain mapping by stimulating electrodes. This is called *extraoperative brain mapping*. This is not a painful test. Only the number and location of the electrodes that were placed on the brain's surface limit the completeness of the final map. The second stage of surgery, which may be several days later, is when the surgeon performs a second operation and removes the abnormal brain tissue using the information gathered from the electrical recordings and the brain mapping. The electrodes are removed at the same time.

As the name implies, a three-stage surgery is composed of three stages. The first stage again involves craniotomy and placement of the electrodes. Seizures are captured. The brain is mapped, and resection is

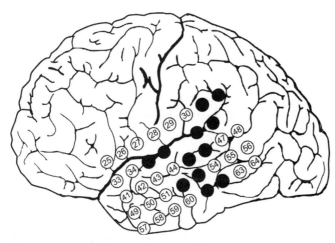

**Figure 16a    Language mapping of the brain—black circles on the grid signify language centers of the brain.**

planned. During the second stage, removal of the abnormal brain tissue or disconnection is done, but some additional electrodes are placed around the margins of the previous surgical cavity, or old electrodes are left behind and the scalp is closed. The idea behind

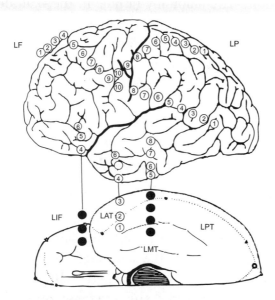

**Figure 16b    Seizure foci on intracranial mapping—black circles on different electrode points on the strips depict different seizure foci.**

*151*

leaving the electrodes is to screen whether there are any additional abnormal foci in the brain causing residual seizures. The patient is sent to the epilepsy monitoring unit, and the patient's intracranial EEG is recorded. Additional resections may be done during the third stage, and the electrodes are removed. This three-stage surgery is done infrequently for very complicated cases with multiple foci or previous failed epilepsy surgery.

## 83. What is an extratemporal surgery?

Surgery performed in any other lobe than the temporal lobe is referred to as extratemporal surgery. Extratemporal surgeries are more frequently performed with advancing technology and precision techniques. These constitute about one fourth of the surgical procedures for epilepsy. Frontal lobe surgeries are the second most common surgeries performed after temporal lobe resections. A craniotomy (a hole in the skull bone) is done to insert the strips, grid, or depth electrodes. The motor, sensory, and language cortex is mapped to reduce potential language or sensorimotor deficits. Cure rates are lower for extratemporal surgery and range from 50% to 70%.

## 84. How is intracranial monitoring done?

**Epileptogenic zone**

Discrete excitogenic area of the cortex believed to be the "seizure focus".

Intracranial EEG is one of the invasive EEG recordings that is done before the epilepsy surgery. It involves putting electrodes on the surface of the brain as close as possible to the region of interest. It gives valuable information about the **epileptogenic zone**, the area involved in the seizures, and abnormal electrical network surrounding the seizure focus. The intracranial EEG measures the activity of a small group of neurons, unlike the scalp EEG, which measures electrical activity from millions of neurons. The scalp EEG is prone to distortion from interference with the skull bone, brain fluid, or underlying skin.

Different types of electrodes are used to record the intracranial EEG. These are called subdural strips (Figure 17), grid (Figure 18), and depth electrodes. Subdural electrodes are arranged in a strip and a large grid. A strip may have 4 to 10 electrode contact points, whereas a grid covers a larger surface area and can have as many as 64 electrode contact points. These are metal electrodes that are imbedded in plastic. The grid is placed after removing the skull bone. The grid implantation is helpful when the seizure focus is believed to be in one lobe. Sometimes it is hard to determine whether the seizure focus is on the right or the left side of the brain. In such cases, a survey study is done with **bilateral strips** to identify the side of ori-

**Bilateral strips**

Placement of strips covering both hemispheres. A procedure is done to find out if there is a partial focus.

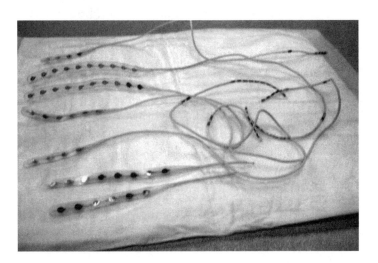

**Figure 17    Strips.**

*153*

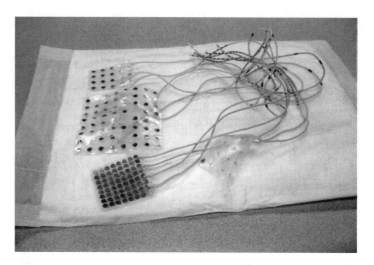

**Figure 18    Grids.**

gin of seizures. This requires burr holes on both sides of the brain, and the strips are placed beneath the dura. Seizures are captured, and the side where the seizure first starts is determined. The depth electrodes can be placed over the area of interest, although the region recorded using these is limited. The main advantage of putting depth electrodes is that you can get access to deep structures of the brain; however, the placement requires brain penetration. Depth electrode placement is associated with increased chance of infection and hemorrhage in the brain.

The cortex can be stimulated using the same electrodes before surgery. This is called extraoperative brain mapping. The seizure map and the brain map revealing the important motor, sensory, and language areas help the neurosurgeon navigate the resection of the seizure focus without compromising the vital areas of the brain (see Figure 18).

## 85. You said that the epilepsy surgery requires removal of the scar tissue from my temporal lobe. What about the scar tissue left from the surgery itself? What evidence do we have that surgery cures epilepsy?

Epilepsy surgery has a good surgical outcome in well-selected cases that are performed by well-trained neurosurgeons. Dr. Samuel Wiebe did a randomized study comparing epilepsy surgery to medical treatment in 80 patients with medically refractory temporal lobe epilepsy. Half of the study group (40 patients) received standard medical treatment, and the other 40 patients underwent immediate presurgical evaluation and surgery. After 1 year, 58% of the patients who underwent surgery had not experienced a complex partial seizure (a seizure that impairs consciousness), and 38% had not experienced any seizures, including auras. In contrast, only 8% of the patients treated with medications were free of complex partial seizures, and 3% had no seizures. For the patients treated with surgery who continued to have some seizures, seizures were less frequent than in the other group, but the severity was similar. The surgical group had a better quality of life compared with the medical group. About 55% of patients were working or studying in the surgical arm versus 36% in the medical arm. A small number of patients suffered from cognitive side effects, and 55% reported a nondisabling defect in a small part of their visual fields.

The epilepsy surgery targets removal of all of the abnormal electrical network area. All of the electrodes are placed in the brain, which shows involvement in the seizure onset, or very frequent electrical discharges are tried to be resected limited by areas, which serve important functions (eloquent cortex). Even those areas are transected, and their normal nerve pathway is disrupted, which allows disruption of seizure spread. This degree of precision and sophisticated state-of-the-art surgery limits the chances of recurrence from the scar tissue.

## 86. What are the complications of epilepsy surgery?

State-of-the-art technology is applied to perform the safest and least invasive epilepsy surgery. Success rates for epilepsy surgery are constantly improving, with advances in preoperative assessment and better technology employed during surgery; however, proper patient selection and a meticulous presurgical noninvasive workup are the cornerstones of successful surgery. Careful screening of patients maximizes seizure freedom and minimizes the postoperative deficits.

**Neurosurgery**

Surgery that is carried out for the treatment of conditions of the nervous system.

Needless to say, epilepsy surgery is major **neurosurgery**. The risks vary from bleeding, infection, hemorrhage, and stroke even to death.

Permanent complications associated with this surgery are very low. Death is rare and ranges from 0.1% to 1.0%, and permanent unexpected morbidity (unanticipated complications such as vision loss, paralysis, and loss of speech or fine motor skills) is less then 1%. When the dominant hemisphere is resected, temporary language difficulties are seen in 10%; however, these usually resolve. An upper **quadrantanopsia** (partial upper peripheral vision loss) is expected in large temporal resections but is seen in less than one fourth of the patients. Memory impairment rarely occurs from temporal lobectomies because it is avoided by preoperative testing of language and memory function.

*Quadrantanopsia*
Defect in the peripheral vision or a visual field defect in the right or left quadrant.

The recovery period varies from individual to individual. The length of hospital stay also varies, depending on the specific procedure performed. Most people can resume normal activities within 4 to 8 weeks after the surgery.

It is critical for the patient and family to have realistic expectations of the results of the surgery. Epilepsy surgery may be **curative** or **palliative**. Curative refers to a complete or significant chance of seizure freedom. In complicated cases, the surgery may be chosen as a palliative procedure. The palliative approach is chosen for difficult surgical cases where surgical outcome is not expected to be seizure freedom; however, it still provides a significant reduction in seizure burden and is aimed to improve the overall quality of life.

*Curative*
Curses epilepsy.

*Palliative*
Not meant to cure the medical condition but provides significant relief.

Your epileptologist and neurosurgeon are able to predict the surgical outcome only roughly (i.e., to give you the rough percentage of seizure freedom after the surgery). After surgery, some patients become completely seizure free, especially with benign lesions on the brain MRI. Others have no improvement at all. Many people fall between these two extremes, having fewer seizures or seizures that are less intense or requiring less medication. Jerome Engel had classified the surgical outcome into four different classes.

Class I: Free of disabling seizures
Class II: Rare disabling seizures ("almost seizure free")
Class III: Worthwhile improvement
Class IV: No worthwhile improvement

Usually antiepileptics are tapered slowly if patients continue to remain seizure free. Patients may experience adjustment, behavioral, or cognitive problems after the surgery.

One of the greatest disappointments after epilepsy surgery is the recurrence of the seizures after seizure freedom for a short period or immediately after surgery. It does not mean, however, that seizures cannot be under control again. Seizures may return because of provoking factors such as brain swelling after the surgery, medical illness, alcohol provocation, increased physical or mental stress, noncompliance with medications on the part of the patient, or a sudden drop in the doses.

## 87. How long will I stay in the hospital after the epilepsy surgery? Will you stop anticonvulsants after the surgery?

Most patients are kept in the intensive care unit for 24 to 48 hours after the epilepsy surgery. Patients are able to resume their normal activities within 3 to 8 weeks. Physical, social, and emotional support may be needed. Antiepileptics are not stopped completely after the surgery. Patients need not be on polypharmacy, and doses may be reduced. Patients may experience adjustment problems and difficulty meeting the new expectations as some enjoy their seizure control. This may require antidepressants, psychotherapy, or individual or group therapy.

## 88. How much will the epilepsy surgery cost?

Brain surgery is very complex, and some complicated cases definitely require adequate brain coverage, the use of sophisticated technology, careful brain mapping, and several other challenges. The cost may range from $50,000 to more than $250,000.

## 89. What is a vagal nerve stimulator?

A vagal nerve stimulator is another form of surgical treatment that can be tried when (1) medications fail, (2) the patient does not wish to have resective surgery, and (3) epilepsy surgery is too risky because of other medical conditions.

The vagal nerve stimulator (Figure 19) manufactured by Ciceroni's was first approved in the United States in 1997 for partial seizures. It was first used in 1988. This device is made of titanium and generates no immune

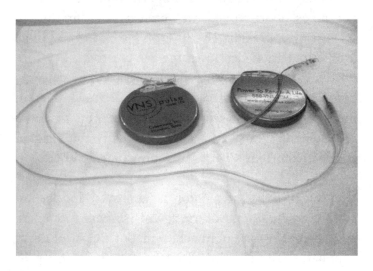

**Figure 19    Vagal nerve stimulator.**

response. The vagus nerve (cranial nerve X) conveys signals between the brain and internal organs such as heart, stomach, intestine, and lungs. The left vagal nerve (a large nerve in the neck) is stimulated by a programmable signal generator into the chest cavity. The left vagus nerve is always selected because the right vagus nerve richly supplies the heart and can have deleterious effects on the heart on its stimulation. The exact mechanism of how the vagal nerve stimulator works is not clear. It sends regular small impulses of electrical energy to the brain via the vagus nerve. Hypothetically, the vagal nerve stimulator prevents seizures by desynchronizing the electrical discharges. The electrical energy is delivered by a battery, which is inserted in the chest wall beneath the skin. The stimulation current intensity, current delivery frequency, and the duration that the current is delivered vary from individual to individual. Every few minutes, electrical impulses stimulate the vagus nerve for a few seconds. Patients and families are instructed to swipe a magnet over the battery if the patient feels an aura or the family witnesses the seizure coming. Swiping of the magnet helps abort/reduce the intensity or duration of seizure in approximately 30% of the patients. High-level stimulation decreases the seizure frequency to a greater extent than low-level stimulation. The percentage of patients with more than a 50% seizure reduction improved with time from 23% at 3 months to about 43% over 3 years. Self-activation with the magnet aborts or shortens seizures in approximately 30%.

The vagal nerve stimulator is approved for use in adults and children over the age of 12 years. Complete seizure control is seldom achieved, but the vagal nerve stimulator may reduce seizure frequency, intensity, or duration of the seizures. Patients may not completely come off antiepileptics but are able to reduce the doses of their antiepileptics and notice significant improvement in their quality of life.

## 90. How long will it take to implant the vagal nerve stimulator?

The surgery takes about 1 or 2 hours. The device consists of a pulse generator and electrodes (see Figure 19). Two incisions are made, one in the chest wall below the collarbone or the armpit and the other in the neck to get access to the left vagus nerve. The pulse generator (10.3-mm thick, 38 gm) is like a pacemaker device that is placed in a surgically created pocket under the skin of the patient's chest wall. The surgeon then threads a plastic tube containing the electrodes from the neck to the generator in the chest. The silicone-coated electrodes are then wrapped around the vagus nerve. The procedure is done under local or general anesthesia, it is mostly done as an outpatient procedure.

## 91. Will I experience an electrical shock every time the nerve is stimulated? What are the side effects of the vagal nerve stimulator?

The vagal nerve stimulator is tolerated very well. The side effects of stimulation may be a tingling feeling in the throat, hoarseness of the voice, cough, or mild breathing problems. Patients may experience tingling or pain in the throat at a higher current intensity. In such an event, the current intensity may be reduced. Most of the side effects are reduced or eliminated with parameter adjustments. The vagal nerve stimulator has no side effects (such as sedation, depression, fatigue, dizziness, weight gain, or memory or sexual problems) that are common with the use of the antiepileptic drugs. It has no interactions with the antiepileptics and does not have compliance issues. Patients and families feel that the situation is under their control to some extent, because they can swipe the magnet.

## 92. What is the cost of this device?

Vagal nerve stimulator therapy costs about $20,000. This includes the cost of the device and the surgery. Medicare and Medicaid and many other insurance carriers cover the cost. The manufacturer (Cyberonics) also provides special assistance to those patients with inadequate medical coverage. The initial frequent follow-up visits requiring careful programming also add to the cost.

## 93. What should I expect after vagal nerve stimulator implantation?

The stimulation settings have to be programmed in the computer. Some epilepsy centers start the stimulation immediately after the surgery. Some wait until the next office visit. A typical parameter setting is 30 seconds on and 5 minutes off. This can be done with the help of the computer, special software, and a programming band. Several follow-up visits may be required. This may be every 2 weeks initially. A patient with the vagal nerve stimulator device should visit the physician at least every 6 months. Caregivers need to be trained as well. This is important in patients who experience no auras or who are mentally disabled. The battery is checked at each visit. Some of the newer models can have a battery life of up to 10 years. The battery life is also dependent on the frequency at which the current is delivered. Program adjustments are done in a few minutes and are painless. The medical staff swipes the magnet to test whether the battery is working properly. It is important to bring to your physician's notice the side effects that you may be experiencing. The device can even be removed in case it has been ineffective or infected. The battery can be replaced using local anesthesia and incision again only in the chest wall. A patient wears the magnet attached to a strap. By swiping the magnet over the pulse generator, the patient or the family member can deliver an extra current in between the cycles. The magnet can also be permanently strapped to the pulse generator to turn the device off, in case there is no improvement or intolerable side effects. The device can be transiently turned off during eating or public speaking to avoid swallowing problems or hoarseness of voice, respectively.

The magnet should be handled carefully, because it can break if dropped on hard surfaces. It can be worn on the wrist as a wristband or clipped to the belt. It should not be stored near the television, microwave ovens, computers, or other magnets. MRIs cannot be obtained in patients with the vagal nerve stimulator device. The vagal nerve stimulator can be explanted if it gets infected or has been proven unsuccessful in controlling the seizures.

The improvement in seizures after vagal nerve stimulator implantation may not be immediate but may be slow and steady. One third of patients show significant improvement, and one third show subtle improvement, whereas the other third may have the same seizure frequency as before the surgery. Studies have demonstrated that patients feel better overall. Their seizures may not be so intense or prolonged; they may have a short postictal period and better memory and mood and may be going to the emergency room less often. The vagal nerve stimulator has far less complications than epilepsy surgical resection. There is about 50% seizure reduction in about 30% to 50% of patients. Patients with vagal nerve stimulator implantation need to maintain the device. This includes having the frequency, duration of stimulation, and the battery checked. With new models, the battery needs to be replaced every 6 to 10 years.

| | |
|---|---|
| Model 100 (version B) | 4–5 years |
| Model 100 (version C) | 6–7 years |
| Model 101 | 9–10 years |
| Model 102 | 8.4 years |
| Model 102R | 8.4 years |

Surgical complications are rare. Complications include infection, wire lead erosion through the skin, or vocal cord paralysis (rare).

## 94. What is transmagnetic stimulation?

In this type of electromagnetic therapy, an insulated coil is placed against the head. The stimulating coil consists of a tightly wound and well-insulated copper coil. A brief magnetic field induced from the coil results in a secondary electrical field that circulates in the opposite direction to the magnetic field. The strength of the electrical field is directly proportional to the first derivative of the magnetic flux over time:

The more rapid the change in magnetic field, the higher is the intensity of the secondary electric field and nervous stimulation. Magnetic stimulation is preferred over electrical stimulation because of its ability to penetrate tissues regardless of electrical resistance.

**Transcranial magnetic stimulation** has been used in experimental studies to treat depression, epilepsy, and other diseases. It is believed that particular areas of the brain can be stimulated by using high-frequency (1 Hz) repetitive transcranial magnetic stimulation. Recently, it has been demonstrated that low-frequency repetitive transcranial magnetic stimulation ($< 1$ Hz) may also inhibit these areas. Most commercially available stimulators can produce stimulations at a rate as high as 5 to 50 Hz. It is hypothesized that if one could locate the area of hyperexcitability of the brain responsible for the disease it could be inhibited.

*Transcranial magnetic stimulation*

In this type of electromagnetic therapy, an insulated coil is placed against the head, and an electrical current generates a magnetic field into the brain.

## 95. What is stereotactic ablation and deep brain stimulation therapy?

Stereotactic lesions of deep cerebral structures for epilepsy control have generally had poor results and were essentially abandoned years ago. Brain stimulation is just beyond the cutting edge in the treatment of epilepsy. The exact mechanism of how stimulation works is not entirely clear. The current hypothesis is that low-frequency stimulations have an excitatory effect, and high-frequency stimulations have an inhibitory effect. There are two ways of stimulating the brain. One is direct stimulation of the seizure focus. The second is to stimulate other areas that are believed to participate in the propagation of seizures through abnormal networks. High-frequency stimulations ($>$

100 Hz) reduce the firing of neurons that inactivates the seizure focus and inhibits the abnormal electrical network pathways that play a vital role in seizure propagation, hyperexcitation, and synchronization of electrical discharges.

Stimulation devices can be open loop or closed loop. In "open-loop" devices, the brain is stimulated in a continuous or cyclical manner, whereas in "closed-loop" devices, the device recognizes the impending or ongoing seizure and provides stimulus only under acute settings. The long-term effects of high-frequency stimulation are unclear. It is more palatable that using a closed-loop device delivering a current at or around the time of seizure is a better approach than using an open-loop device. Studies done on the patients in this field are still in their infancy. It is not clear where these devices should be implanted and what should be the stimulation parameters.

## 96. What are implantable neurostimulators?

An implantable neurostimulator is a small electronic device that is implanted in the skull near the seizure focus. Tiny screws hold the device securely in place. The neurosurgeon places up to two electrodes within the brain near the seizure focus. A modified laptop computer then analyzes the electrical activity revealed by the neurostimulator. The device is then programmed to recognize the patient's seizure activity. If the neurostimulator detects abnormal electrical or seizure-like activity, it sends an electrical stimulus to stop it. This device is being studied at the Medical College of Georgia for its use in the future. If the implantable neurostimulator is proven to be safe and effective, it may benefit many epilepsy patients in the future.

## 97. What is a neuroprosthesis?

Neurosurgeons implant an electrode into the brain that could either predict or recognize the occurrence of seizures or abnormal neurobiological signals. The device has seizure detection capabilities and a delivery system to inject medication to the specific areas of the brain tissue or the surrounding brain fluid where seizures would have originated.

Because the drug would be delivered directly to the appropriate area(s) of the brain, the amount needed to control the seizures would be 100 or 1,000 times smaller than if the medication were taken orally. Thus, this method could drastically reduce the side effects of current antiepileptics. The ability to deliver a small dose of medication directly to the affected area of the brain obviates the need to take larger doses of antiepileptics. This device can also facilitate the use of drugs that are good anticonvulsants but cannot cross the blood–brain barrier to exert their action. This could open the door to new medications, not just for epilepsy, but also for several other brain disorders.

## 98. Would you recommend gamma-knife surgery (GKS) for epilepsy? How does it work?

A gamma knife is an instrument that uses a concentrated radiation dose from cobalt-60 sources to damage abnormal tissue. The accuracy of this tool lies in about 201 beams of radiation that intersect in the damaged abnormal area. These beams are focused on the target area, and only abnormal tissue is destroyed. This technique is ideal for small lesions where this radiosurgical instrument creates a small, well-defined, and precise volume lesion. This technique minimizes the negative effects on the surrounding normal tissue. This surgical approach does not need any physical entry into the brain and thereby reduces the chances of brain swelling, fluid shifts, infection, hemorrhage, and stroke. Treatment with the gamma knife requires a team approach. It relies highly on the expertise of the neurosurgeon, radiation oncologist, and radiation physicist.

Lars Leksell originally developed the gamma knife in 1968. It has emerged as the most technically advanced stereotactic radiosurgery of our time after decades of in-depth research and experimental trials. It was initially used to treat brain tumors and blood vessel abnormalities (**arteriovenous malformations** and cavernomas of the brain).

*Arteriovenous malformations*
A tangle of blood vessels in the brain that can bleed and commonly cause seizures.

There are definite advantages of this technique. The surgical complications are reduced. The entire procedure is performed without an incision. It is a painless procedure that can be performed under local anesthesia and mild sedation. It avoids complications of general anesthesia. The hospital stay after the procedure is drastically reduced. The conventional neurosurgery means prolonged hospital stay or rehabilitation, which dramatically increases the costs. Patients can be discharged the same day and can resume their activities immediately. It may be a reasonable option for small lesions or when the patient's age or other medical illnesses are the major risk factor for conventional neurosurgery.

It has been tried in patients with mesial temporal lobe epilepsy, **cavernous angioma** (blood vessel abnormality), and hypothalamic hematomas (tumor in the hypothalamus) or other benign tumors. In March 1993, a patient with mesial temporal lobe epilepsy was treated in Marseille, France. The Regis group studied the outcome of gamma knife surgery in a relatively large series of patients with temporal lobe epilepsy (Regis J, Bartolomei F, Rey M., *Journal Neurosurg*, 2000; 93[Suppl 3]:141-6). Almost all cases were associated with space-occupying lesions. In their series, they had a 2-year follow-up available for more than 16 of 25 patients entering the study. About 13 of 16 patients (81%) were seizure free, and two had improved. This was comparable to traditional surgery. They observed a median delay of 10.5 months in seizure control after gamma knife surgery. Three patients noted visual problems (visual field deficit) after the GKS. No permanent neurological deficits and morbidity or mortality were observed. Further long-term follow-up is required. There are ongoing U.S. multicenter and European trials funded by the National Institute of Health to define the role of GKS further in the field of epilepsy.

*Cavernous angioma*

One of the types of malformations of the blood vessels in the brain. It can cause seizures, stroke symptoms, hemorrhages, and headache. It occurs relatively frequently in children.

**Presurgical Evaluation and Epilepsy Surgery**

## 99. What can I do to improve my quality of life when living with epilepsy?

Physical health, mental health, and social health are three different aspects that need to be addressed in any chronic medical condition such as epilepsy. Patients should not only be asked about their seizure control or the side effects of antiepileptics. The consultation with the epileptologist should go beyond these very basic questions. How is the patient doing overall? There may be several psychosocial issues (Table 27), such as fear and embarrassment of seizures. Patients may be living with a low self-esteem, as they lose their independence or ability to drive. Some patients have to rethink their goals in life. The patient's own health perceptions vary and are important in deciding treatment strategies.

Patients should honestly maintain a seizure diary that lists all kinds of seizures. The medications should be taken to enforce seizure control. If you experience any side effects of medications, you should discuss these with your neurologist or epileptologist instead of skipping doses. Your physician can always work with you and switch to another antiepileptic. Both patients and physicians should be more forthcoming in exploring other important coexisting issues with seizures such as

**Table 27    Psychosocial Aspects of Epilepsy**

- Driving
- Independent living
- Insurance
- Economic
- Employment
- Dating
- Marriage
- Decreased libido
- Planning family
- Social stigma
- School problems
- Social intermingling
- Lifestyle restrictions
- Depression, anxiety, paranoia
- Fear of next seizure, physical injuries, or death during a seizure
- Cognitive issues

hyposexuality, anxiety, depression, or other cognitive (judgment, information processing time, abstract thinking, memory, and language skills) deficits.

## 100. Where can I go for more information on the subject?

This small handbook cannot answer all of the questions you might have. I have tried to give you a list of resources that will enable you to find some other answers. The Appendix also specifies some of the well-known organizations, websites, and other reliable sources of information. A lot of these organizations are happy to provide you with related reading materials. These websites also have more information about the scholarships programs and occupational, vocational, educational, and other support programs offered to patients with epilepsy. Enjoy!

# *Appendix: National Epilepsy Resources*

**Epilepsy Foundation**
4351 Garden City Drive
Landover, MD 20785
Phone: (410) 828-7700 or (800) 332-1000
Web site: www.epilepsyfoundation.org
The Epilepsy Foundation is a national organization that serves people that are affected by seizures through research, education, advocacy, and services provided at over 60 affiliates nationwide.

**www.epilepsy.com**
This Web site is provided by the Epilepsy Project. It educates patients and their families about newly diagnosed epilepsy and medically refractory seizures.

**Exceptional Parent**
www.exceptionalparent.com
This provides information, support, ideas, encouragement, and
outreach for parents and families of children with disabilities
and the professionals who work with them.

**Parents Against Childhood Epilepsy, Inc.**
7 East 85th Street, Suite A
New York, NY 10028
Phone: (212) 665-PACE
Web site: www.paceusa.org

**The Epilepsy Institute**
257 Park Avenue, South, 4th Floor
New York, NY 10010
Phone: (212) 677-8550
Web site: www.epilepsyinstitute.org
The Epilepsy Institute provides comprehensive educational and
social services to patients and their families. It offers specialized
supported employment, state-certified counselors, and day
habilitation programs. Several recreational programs, such as
weekend socialization programs or summer camps, are orga-
nized. This institute also offers educational services, information, and referral services to patients with epilepsy. All
programs are free or low cost.

**Doctor's Guide: Epilepsy**
Web site: www.docguide.com/news/content.nsf/
PatientResAllCateg/Epilepsy?OpenDocument

**Emedicine: Epilepsy**
Web site: http://www.emedicine.com/aaem/topic183.htm

**http://www.epilepsy.com/epilepsy/**
This Web site is designed to empower patients and families who
are coping with epilepsy by providing information and support
resources to understand and manage the disease better.

**MEDLINEplus Health Information: Epilepsy**
This Web site includes overviews of epilepsy, news, clinical trials,
diagnostic tests, and disease management. Plenty of information is available on nutrition, research, treatment, and specific

conditions such as pregnancy and epilepsy. Special sections are
dedicated to children, seniors, teenagers, and women.
http://www.nlm.nih.gov/medlineplus/epilepsy.html

### Merck Manual Home Edition: Seizure Disorders

This detailed overview of seizure disorders is presented in this
section of the Merck patient publication. In-text links will
direct the reader to related topics, glossary entries, and associated charts and diagrams.
http://www.merck.com/pubs/mmanual_home/sec6/73.html

### National Institute of Neurology and Stroke: Epilepsy Information Page

Answers are given to frequently asked questions about epilepsy.
An extensive listing of related organizations and links to rele-
vant publications are provided at the conclusion of the text.
www.ninds.nih.gov/health_and_medical/disorders/epilepsy.htm

### http://seizures.net

This is sponsored by North Pacific Epilepsy Research.
Seizures.net offers a range of resources for both professional
and public audiences. A number of Spanish resources are also
available.

### WHO: Epilepsy: Scientific and Medical Advances

Sponsored by the World Health Organization, this fact sheet
presents information on basic and clinical research in epilepsy.
The purpose and focal points of both basic and clinical research
are examined. Additional topics include diagnostic research,
pharmacotherapy, and surgical therapy. A listing of key points
from the text is provided at the bottom of the page.
http://www.who.int/inf-fs/en/fact167.html

### Epiweb.org: Treatment

The extensive chart available on this page provides information
on over 20 anticonvulsant medications. The chart includes
generic and brand name, producer, indications, common side
effects, and remarks. Several drugs include links to product
information. The second chart on the page offers similar
information on alternative therapies such as herbal medicine,
aromatherapy, and acupuncture.
http://www.epiweb.org/treatment.html

**Johns Hopkins Epilepsy Center: Ketogenic Diet**

The basic protocol for the ketogenic diet, as well as information on how it works, is presented. Contacts for obtaining additional information are provided.

http://www.neuro.jhmi.edu/Epilepsy/keto.html

**Finding a Cure for Epilepsy and Seizures**

NYU Comprehensive Epilepsy Center/NYU Tuberous Sclerosis Center

403 East, 34th Street, 4th Floor

New York, NY 10016

Phone: (212) 779-2080

Fax: (212) 779-2331

Web site: www.nyufaces.org

This organization provides free educational conferences, seminars, and several social events for children and teens, summer camp scholarships, respite care program, and support groups for parents. It is promoting research into neuroprosthesis, magnetic stimulation, biofeedback, and new surgical procedures. Faces also support the NYU Tuberous Sclerosis Center.

**Resources for Children with Special Needs**

116 East 16th Street, 5th Floor

New York, NY 10003

Phone: (212) 677-4650

E-mail: info@resourcesnyc.org

Web site: www.resourcenyc.org

Resources for Children with Special Needs is a comprehensive, independent, nonprofit organization, referral, advocacy, training, and support center for New York City parents and professionals who are looking for all types of programs and services for children from birth to 21 years with learning, developmental, emotional, and physical disabilities. Resources are designated by the US Department of Education as one of a national network of more than 100 parent training and information centers.

**The Special Education Resource Center**

25 Industrial Park Road

Middletown, CT 06457-1520

Phone: (860) 632-1485

Web site: www.ctserc.org

### The Epilepsy Institute Travel Day Camp
New York, NY
Phone: (212) 677-8550
Contact: Pam Conford, Executive Director

### American Airlines "Miles for Kids in Need"
Contact: Program Administration
Phone: (817) 963-8158
Fax: (817) 931-6890
Web site: www.americanairlines.com

### The National Epilepsy Foundation J. Kiffin Penry Travel Assistance Program
Phone: (800) EFA-1000
Web site: www.efa.org
The Epilepsy Foundation offers a limited number of travel assistance grants, up to $1,500 each (over a 2-year period) for people who must travel for specialized epilepsy care or testing.

### Families and Advocates Partnership for Education
PACER Center
8161 Normandale Boulevard
Minneapolis, MN 55437
Phone: (952) 838-9000
Fax: (952) 838-0199
E-mail: fape@fape.org
Web site: www.fape.org
FAPE aims to improve the educational outcomes for children with disabilities. It links families, advocates, and self-advocates for communication about the Individuals with Disabilities Education Act.

### Learning Disabilities Online
Web site: www.idonline.org
This Web site provides valuable information for parents and teachers who are working with children with learning disabilities.

### *Negotiating the Special Education Maze: A Guide for Parents & Teachers*, 3rd Edition, by Winifred Anderson
This book is an introduction to special education law and the process of getting services for your child.

### Sensory Integration Network

Web site: www.sinetwork.org/home/index.html

This is a Web site for parents, teachers, and therapists on sensory integration problems. It contains useful pamphlets that can be downloaded to explain dysfunctional sensory integration to teachers.

### Wrightslaw

Web site: www.wrightslaw.com

This comprehensive website is dedicated to special education about the rights the children and parents have and how parents can advocate for their children.

### American Epilepsy Society

638 Prospect Avenue

Hartford, CT 06105

Phone: (860) 586-7505

Web site: http://www.aesnet.org

The AES Web site features a searchable member directory where you can find epilepsy specialists near you.

### National Association of Epilepsy Centers

5775 Wayzata Boulevard

Minneapolis, MN 55415

Phone: (612) 525-4526

Web site: http://www.naecepilepsy.org

The NAEC is a nonprofit organization whose members include more than 50 specialized centers.

### Pharmaceutical Research and Manufacturers of America

1100 15th Street, NW

Washington, DC 20005

Web site: www.helpingpatients.org

PhRMA has information on prescription drug patient assistance programs on their Web site.

### Vocational Rehabilitation Offices

For the office nearest you, call (800) 222-JOBS (5627).

### JobTech Employment Program

This is the most comprehensive employment program developed by the Epilepsy Foundation.

## JobTalk

This is a new on-line feature that includes a monthly chat session in which experts answer questions about employment-related issues. For more information on Jobtalk, please go to www.epilepsyfoundation.org.

## Federation Employment and Guideline Services

315 Hudson Street
New York, NY 10013
Phone: (212) 366-8246
Web site: www.fegs.org

## International Center for the Disabled

340 East 24th Street
New York, NY 10010
Phone: (212) 585-6000

## National Organization on Disability

910 Sixteenth Street, NW, Suite 600
Washington, DC 20006
Phone: (202) 293-5960
Web site: www.nod.org

## The Job Accommodation Network

P.O. Box 6080
Morgantown, WV 26506
Phone: (800) 526-7234
Web site: www.jan.wvu.edu

## The Internet Resources for Special Children

This is a nonprofit search site that was put together by the parents of a disabled child to communicate information relating to the needs of children with disabilities.
www.irsc.org

## The Epilepsy Book Store

Books can be ordered on-line and shipped worldwide.
http://www.wellnessbooks.com/epilepsy/

Appendix

**UCLA Neurosurgery**
The neuroscience teaching program at UCLA with the Clinical
Neuroscience Program ranks in the top 10 in America.
http://www.neurosurgery.medsch.ucla.edu/

**Beach Park**
This is the British Epilepsy Association children's home page.
http://www.epilepsy.org.uk/kids/index.html

**Little Poss Home Page**
http://www.littleposs.com/

**Neuroscience for Kids**
This is recommended for elementary and secondary school
students and teachers who would like to learn more about
the nervous system.
http://faculty.washington.edu/chudler/neurok.html

**Epilepsy Foundation of America**
The Epilepsy Foundation of America provides information and
referral for women with epilepsy. By contacting the Foundation
or local affiliates, physicians, and lay persons may obtain a
series of fact sheets on issues of concern in women with
epilepsy.
Phone: (800) EFA-1000
Web site: www.efa.org

**North American Pregnancy Registry**
This is a prospective national registry that is established to identify teratogenic risks of antiepileptic drugs. Pregnant women
should contact the registry before they have a diagnostic ultrasound.
Phone: (888) 233-2334

**WomensHealthChannel: Epilepsy in Pregnancy**
Issues associated with maternal epilepsy during pregnancy are
discussed in detail in this article from the WomensHealth
Channel. The site presents an overview of the topic with general information and material on the incidence and the use of
antiepileptic medications during pregnancy.
http://www.womenshealthchannel.com/seizures/index.shtml

**American Foundation for Urologic Disease**
1000 Corporate Boulevard, Suite 410
Linthicum, MD 21090
Phone: (410) 689-3990
E-mail: impotence@afud.org
Web site: www.impotence.org

**American Urological Association**
1000 Corporate Boulevard
Linthicum, MD 21090
Phone: (866) 746-4282 or (410) 689-3700
E-mail: aua@auanet.org
Web site: www.auanet.org

**American Association of Sex Educators, Counselors, and Therapists**
P.O. Box 5488
Richmond, VA 23220-0488
Web site: www.aasect.org

# *Glossary*

**Ablation:** A procedure that removes damaged tissues using heat sources.

**Absence seizure:** A generalized seizure involving a brief interruption of consciousness. The person briefly stares blankly and the eyelids may flutter. This is also called petit mal.

**Acquired epileptic aphasia:** Regression of language after normal language development; this condition is associated with seizures and behavioral problems.

**Acupuncture:** A Chinese tradition where fine needles are used to stimulate specific areas along certain meridians that balance the energy flow in that area.

**Adrenocorticotrophic hormone:** A hormone that is produced by the master pituitary gland. It stimulates the adrenal gland to secrete corticosteroids that help cells synthesize glucose, metabolize proteins, mobilize free fatty acids and inhibit inflammation in allergic responses.

**Agoraphobia:** An unexplained fear of open spaces.

**Allergic reactions:** Allergic reactions are side effects that occur because an individual is sensitive to the drug. One example is rash. Anyone who experiences an allergic reaction should see a doctor immediately and hold the medicine.

**Alopecia:** Thinning or loss of hair.

**Alpha-fetoprotein:** An antigen present in the human fetus and in diseased conditions in the adult.

**Ambulatory EEG:** A portable type of EEG that allows the electrical activity of the brain to be recorded over a period of several hours or several days. Electrodes are attached to the scalp and a recorder is worn on a belt around the waist. This obviates the need to be in the hospital and person can continue his or her daily activities.

**Amenorrhea:** Absence of regular menstruation or monthly vaginal bleeding in women.

**Anoxia:** A lack of oxygen.

**Antibiotics:** Drugs that fight infections.

**Anticonvulsant:** An antiepileptic drug used to treat seizures.

**Antiepileptics:** Medications used to prevent the spread of seizures in patients with epilepsy.

**Arteriovenous malformation:** A tangle of blood vessels in the brain that can bleed and commonly cause seizures.

**Astrocytoma:** A type of brain tumor that is also the most common type of glioma (tumor of the glial cells, the cells that provide support and protection of the nerve cells of the brain). It is most commonly found in the cerebrum (main part of the brain) and it is most common in adults, particularly middle-aged men.

**Ataxia:** Difficulty walking or balancing.

**Atherosclerosis:** The progressive narrowing and hardening of the arteries over time. This is known to occur with aging, but other risk factors such as high cholesterol, high blood pressure smoking, diabetes, and family history for atherosclerotic disease can hasten this process.

**Atonic seizures:** Generalized seizures causing sudden loss of muscle tone resulting in falls to the ground. Recovery is rapid, but the patient is at a risk of serious injuries to the head or other body parts.

**Auras:** Warnings before a seizure that the patients can recall. This is a sensation—sometimes a strange smell or taste or a twitching in one limb—that may act as a warning that a sei-

zure is going to happen. Auras are actually simple partial seizures and may sometimes occur in isolation, without progressing to a complex partial or tonic–clonic seizure.

**Automatism:** Automatic or altered behavior—typically occuring during a complex partial seizure—lip smacking, rearranging objects, chewing or swallowing movements, fumbling with clothing, and undressing.

**Axon:** Part of a neuron that conducts impulses away from the cell body.

**Basilar migraine:** A migraine associated with complicated symptoms such as, slurred speech, loss of balance, or brief loss of consciousness.

**Benign sleep myoclonus:** A distinctive disorder of sleep in infancy characterized by rhythmic myoclonic jerks (sudden muscle contractions) that occur when the child is asleep and stop when the child is awakened. Sleep myoclonus usually disappears after a few weeks and can be confused with epilepsy.

**Benign rolandic epilepsy:** Age-related benign epilepsy syndrome; categorized as partial epilepsy; patients have nocturnal focal seizures with very abnormal EEG, normal MRI brain and neurological exams.

**Bilateral strips:** Placement of strips covering both hemispheres. A procedure is done to find out if there is a partial focus.

**Brain tumors:** Abnormal proliferation of brain cells, neurons or supporting cells (glia).

**Brainstem:** Lower part of the brain.

**Brand name:** The name given to a drug by the company that manufactures it.

**Catamenial epilepsy:** Seizures that only occur before or during menstruation or at the time of ovulation.

**Catamenial migraine:** Increase in the frequency of migraine attacks in relation to different phases of menstruation.

**Cavernous angioma:** One type of malformations of the blood vessels in the brain. It can cause seizures, stroke symptoms, hemorrhages, and headache. It occurs relatively frequently in children.

**Cell body:** The main part of the cell around the nucleus, used in reference to neurons.

**Central nervous system:** The portion of the vertabrate nervous system consisting of the brain and spinal cord.

**Cerebellar atrophy:** Shrinkage of the lower part of the brain called the cerebellum, which is important for the coordination of movement and balance.

**Cerebral angiogram:** An x-ray of the arteries and veins in the brain. For the test, a contrast dye is passed into the blood vessels through a catheter.

**Childhood absence epilepsy**: Age-related benign generalized epilepsy with very brief clusters of absence seizures, these seizures are also referred to as petit mal seizures.

**Childhood epilepsy with occipital paroxysms:** Benign epilepsy with visual auras and EEG reveals excitation in the occipital lobes. Often confused with migraines.

**Clonic seizures:** Epileptic seizures characterized by jerking movements that involves muscles on both sides of the body.

**Complementary and alernatative medicines:** This is a group of diverse medical and healthcare systems, practices, and products that are not presently considered to be part of conventional medicine.

**Complex febrile seizures:** Seizures occurring in relation to high fever, usually prolonged and may show asymmetric involvement of the body or focal features clinically. These tend to recur more often.

**Complex partial seizures:** Partial seizures where the person's awareness is impaired.

**Compliance:** Taking medication as prescribed (i.e., the correct dose at the correct time).

**Computerized axial tomography (CAT) scan:** A brain scan showing anatomy of the brain using x-rays.

**Convulsive syncope:** A brief loss of consciousness (syncope) associated with mild convulsions and stiffening.

**Corpus callosotomy:** Disconnection of corpus callosum.

**Corpus callosum:** A band of nerves that integrates the functions of the two halves of the brain.

**Cortex:** The outer layer of an organ or other body structure.

**Cortical dysplasia:** A malformed disorganization of the cerebral cortex.

**Cryptogenic epilepsy:** Epilepsy where the cause of the condition cannot be determined.

**Cyanotic:** Spells that are associated with fear, trauma, and emotional stress. A child stops breathing and turns blue and may have a brief loss of consciousness.

**Deep brain stimulation:** A treatment where a probe or electrode is implanted and used to stimulate a clearly defined, abnormally discharging brain region to block the abnormal activity.

**Delusion:** A false belief.

**Dementia:** Derangement of memory— a loss of previously acquired thinking skills.

**Dendrites:** Part of a neuron that conducts impulses from adjacent cells inward toward the cell body.

**Depression:** Chronic feelings of sadness, despair, and helplessness.

**Depth electrodes:** These are multiple-contact "needles" of polyurethane or other material that are inserted into the brain to help locate the seizure onset intracranially.

**Diabetes mellitus:** Diabetes caused by a relative or absolute deficiency of insulin.

**Diffusion tensor imaging (DTI):** Measures the movement of water in the brain and detects areas where the normal flow of water is disrupted. A disrupted flow of water indicates where there could be an underlying abnormality.

**Disconnection:** Surgical resection of neuronal pathways that connect two areas of the brain.

**Doose syndrome:** A rare disorder with frequent and sudden drop attacks, violent myoclonic jerks, or abrupt loss of muscular tone (i.e., astatic seizures).

**Drop attacks:** A sudden loss of muscle tone resulting in falls and physical injuries. The seizures are brief, generalized and are associated with both atonic or tonic seizures.

**Electrical epileptiform discharges:** An abnormal excitation in the brain referred to as "epilepsy brain waves."

**Electrocardiogram:** The curve traced by an electrocardiograph.

**Electroencephalogram (EEG):** Graphic representation of brain waves revealing the functional status of the brain.

**Encephalitis:** Inflammation of the brain tissue.

**Epilepsia partialis continua:** Continuous seizure activity originating from one side of the brain. Patients may be completely aware of their surroundings. This condition is commonly seen in patients with brain tumors.

**Epilepsy:** A neurological condition where a person has a tendency to have repeated seizures, more than two that are unprovoked.

**Epileptiform discharges:** Abnormal waves in an EEG in patients with epilepsy that indicate signs of excitation in the brain.

**Epileptogenic:** Having the ability to induce epilepsy.

**Epileptologist:** A neurologist who specializes in epilepsy.

**Erectile dysfunction:** Impairment of achieving erection.

**Estrogen:** A general term for female steroid sex hormones that are secreted by the ovary and responsible for typical female sexual characteristics.

**Febrile convulsions:** Convulsions seen with high fever.

**Febrile seizures:** Seizures in association with high fever.

**Focal seizure:** An older term for a partial seizure. A seizure coming from one discrete focus or part of the brain.

**Focus:** An identified area of the brain from which partial seizures arise.

**Forced normalization:** A relationship between seizure control and psychotic symptoms that exist in some patients with intractable epilepsies.

**Frontal lobe:** The part of the brain that is involved in movement and some aspects of thought, judgment initiation, and abstract thinking.

**Gamma-aminobutyric acid:** A neurotransmitter that inhibits neuronal firing.

**Gamma knife:** A relatively new form of surgery that uses gamma radiation to destroy the part of the brain that the surgeon has identified as being the cause of epilepsy.

**Gamma rays:** Electromagnetic radiation emitted during radioactive decay that have an extremely short wavelength.

**Generalized epilepsy:** Epilepsy characterized by different seizure types, such as, tonic-clonic, clonic, tonic, absence or myoclonic seizures. These are typically not preceded by any aura and show diffuse involvement of the brain on the EEG during the seizure.

**Generalized seizures:** An abnormal electrical activity occuring simultaneously from both sides of the brain.

**Genes:** Hereditary material composed of long strands of four molecules that determine the synthesis of proteins.

**Genetics:** Relating to genes.

**Glutamate:** An excitatory neurotransmitter.

**Gonadotrophin-releasing hormone:** A hormone secreted by the hypothalamus, which in turn provides feedback to the pituitary and gonads.

**Gonads:** Sex glands (ovary and testis where eggs and sperms are produced respectively).

**Grand mal:** A sudden attack or convulsion characterized by generalized muscle spasms and loss of consciousness.

**Grid:** An array of multiple electrodes that is inserted after opening skull bone. It can cover a wider area of brain compared to strips.

**Hemispherectomy:** Disconnects one cerebral hemisphere from the rest of the brain. It is performed only for intractable epilepsy where one side of the brain is functioning poorly.

**Hemispheres:** Two parts of the brain (right and left).

**Hemorrhagic disease of the newborn:** Bleeding in the internal organs of a newborn during the first few days of life. It results from decreased levels of vitamin K, which is an essential factor for blood clotting.

**Hippocampal atrophy:** Shrinkage or volume loss in the hippocampus.

**Hippocampus:** Part of the temporal lobe of the brain that is involved in memory consolidation.

**Homeopathy:** Based on the belief that a disease can be treated with diluted doses of various substances.

**Hydrocephalus:** An enlargement of the head caused by an abnormal buildup of cerebrospinal fluid (liquid that serves as an extra cushion to protect the brain and spine from damage) in the ventricles of the brain. As a result, a person with hydrocephalus may suffer mild to moderate mental retardation.

**Hyperventilation:** Rapid, deep breathing; this technique may provoke epileptiform waves or seizures (especially petit mal seizures) during an EEG recording.

**Hypothalamus:** A region in the brain that controls all the glands and the autonomic nervous system.

**Hypothyroidism:** Insufficient production of thyroid hormone levels in the body.

**Hypoxia:** The prolonged lack of oxygen to the brain.

**Hypsarrhythmia:** A distinctive EEG pattern associated with infantile spasms.

**Ictal:** The period during a seizure.

**Idiopathic epilepsy:** Epilepsy where the cause of the condition is not known but genetic factors are believed to be involved.

**Incontinence:** Involuntary urination

**Infantile spasms:** Clusters of rapid jerks followed by stiffening or jack-knife movements.

**Intracarotid sodium amobarbital procedure:** Also called WADA test, used to localize speech and memory function prior to surgical treatment of temporal lobe seizures.

**Intracranial EEG recording:** EEG recording from intracranial electrodes (electrode grid/strips placed directly on the cortical surface or implanted depth electrode).

**Intractable seizures:** Seizures that do not respond to treatment.

**Ischemia:** The prolonged lack of blood supply to the brain.

**Juvenile absence epilepsy:** Primarily absence seizures with onset near puberty, myoclonic and grand mal seizures are also seen.

**Juvenile myoclonic epilepsy:** A syndrome with onset during teenage years and is characterized by absence, tonic-clonic, and myoclonic seizures.

**Ketogenic diet:** A high-fat diet that is sometimes used to treat severe epilepsy in children.

**Kindling:** A procedure used in animals in which unprovoked seizures can be produced by a series of provoked seizures.

**Lafora disease:** A form of progressive myoclonus epilepsy with psychomotor retardation, seizures (primarily myoclonic or grand mal), and EEG shows occipital spikes. Diagnosis is made with skin biopsy and/or genetic testing.

**Landau Kleffner syndrome:** A rare childhood syndrome where the child has seizures and regression of language.

**Lennox-Gestaut syndrome:** A severe form of epilepsy that usually begins in early childhood and is characterized by frequent seizures of multiple types, mental impairment, and a particular brain wave pattern (a slow spike-and-wave pattern). The seizures are notoriously hard to treat and may lead to falls and injuries.

**Lesionectomy:** Removal of a lesion (pathological or traumatic discontinuity of tissue).

**Libido:** Desire for sex.

**Lupus:** An autoimmune disorder causing inflammation in different organs, such as, the heart and kidneys, as well as the joints and blood vessels.

**Magnetic resonance imaging (MRI):** A brain scan using magnetic field showing details of the structure of the brain in a three-dimensional way.

**Magnetic resonance spectroscopy:** Detection and measurements of resonant spectra of molecules (metabolites) in a tissue sample.

**Magnetic source imaging (MSI):** Superimposition of MEG data on a magnetic resonance image (MRI).

**Magnetoencephalography:** Noninvasive functional brain mapping that localizes electrical activity of the brain by measuring the associated magnetic fields emanating from the brain.

**Medically refractory seizures:** Seizures that are not controlled by medical therapy treatment alone as monotherapy or in combination.

**Meningitis:** Inflammation of the coverings of the brain (meninges).

**Mesial temporal sclerosis:** Subtle scar seen in the temporal lobes in patients with temporal lobe epilepsy due to neuronal loss.

**Mitochondria:** Cellular energy sources.

**Monotherapy:** The use of one drug only in the treatment of any medical illness.

**Mood disorders:** Disturbances of mood such as major depression, mania, or hypomania.

**Multiple sclerosis:** A neurodegenerative condition primarily involving the white matter of the brain.

**Multiple subpial transections:** This procedure is a kind of epilepsy surgery where small cuts are made into the brain's cerebral cortex. This helps to reduce or eliminate seizures arising from important functional areas of the brain where removal of tissue is not possible.

**Myoclonic seizures:** Generalized seizures with brief jerks of a part or the whole body.

**Neurological conditions:** Medical conditions involving the nervous system.

**Neurologist:** A physician who specializes in conditions of the nervous system.

**Neurology:** The medical science that deals with the nervous system and disorders affecting it.

**Neurons:** Building blocks of the brain made up of a cell body, the axon, and the dendrites.

**Neuronal ceroid lipofuscinosis:** A neurodegenerative condition associated with seizures, developmental delays, and blindness.

**Neuropsychiatrists:** Physicians who specialize in neurological conditions that are producing psychiatric symptoms.

**Neuropsychologists:** Physicians who specialize in the relationship between the brain and how individuals think and behave.

**Neuroradiologists:** Specialists who use imaging devices and substances to study the brain.

**Neurosurgery:** Surgery that is carried out for the treatment of conditions of the nervous system.

**Neurosurgeons:** Surgeons who carry out surgery for the treatment of conditions of the nervous system.

**Neurotransmitters:** These are small-molecular-weight compounds that convey messages across a synapse. Some examples of neurotransmitters are acetylcholine, glutamate, gamma-aminobutyric acid, norepinephrine, and serotonin.

**Nocturnal seizures:** Seizures that occur during sleep, usually at night.

**Nonepileptic seizures (NES):** Seizures that are not caused by epilepsy.

**Obsessive-compulsive behavior:** An anxiety disorder characterized by recurrent, persistent obsessions or compulsions. Obsessions are the intrusive ideas, thoughts, or images that are experienced as senseless or repugnant. Compulsions are repetitive, purposeless behavior which the individual generally recognizes as senseless and from which the individual does not

derive pleasure. It may provide a release from tension, however.

**Occipital lobe:** The part of the brain that subserves visual perception.

**Ohtahara's syndrome:** A neurological disorder that affects newborns, usually within the first 3 months of life (most often within the first 10 days) in the form of epileptic seizures. Infants have primarily tonic seizures, but may also experience partial seizures, and occasionally, myoclonic seizures. Ohtahara syndrome is most commonly caused by metabolic disorders or structural damage in the brain, although the cause or causes for many cases cannot be determined. The EEG shows typical changes called "burst suppression" pattern.

**Organelles:** Differentiated structures within a cell that perform specific functions.

**Osteoporosis:** A condition characterized by decrease in bone mass with decreased bone density and enlargement of bone spaces producing brittleness.

**Palliative:** Not meant to cure the medical condition but provides significant relief.

**Pallid syncope:** Often precipitated by trauma, the child becomes limp and extremely pale with very brief loss of consciousness.

**Panic attack:** A sudden onset of panic with no apparent cause.

**Paresthesias:** A sensation of pricking, tingling, or creeping on the skin.

**Parietal lobe:** The part of the brain that is involved in perceiving sensations.

**Parkinson's disease:** A degenerative disorder of the central nervous system characterized by tremor or impaired muscle coordination.

**Paroxysmal:** A sudden outburst or eruption.

**Partial epilepsy:** Epilepsy originating from a part of the cortex.

**Partial seizures:** Seizures where the abnormal electrical activity begins in one part of the brain.

**Petit mal:** *See* absence seizures.

**Phonophobia:** Fear of sounds and noise.

**Photic stimulation:** Stimulation of the brain by flashing light or alternating patterns of light and dark.

**Photon:** A particle that travels at the speed of light.

**Photophobia:** An abnormal or irrational fear of light.

**Photosensitive epilepsy:** A form of epilepsy where seizures are triggered by flickering or flashing light at particular frequencies.

**Photosensitivity:** When seizures are triggered by lights flashing or flickering at particular frequencies and, sometimes, by certain geometric shapes or patterns.

**Pituitary gland:** The master gland of the endocrine system. It is located at the base of the brain.

**Polycystic ovarian syndrome:** A disease that causes an enlarged ovary with cysts on the surface.

**Polytherapy:** The use of more than one drug in the treatment of a medical condition.

**Positron emission tomography (PET):** A 3-dimensional brain scan that gives information about the function and the structure of the brain. It is a nuclear medicine test in which tissue function can be imaged. Damaged tissues have reduced metabolic activity; therefore, gamma radiation from these areas is reduced or absent.

**Positron:** An electrically charged particle that has the opposite charge as an electron. It reacts with an electron to produce gamma rays.

**Postictal psychosis:** A state of psychosis occurring after a seizure. *See* psychosis.

**Posttraumatic epilepsy:** Seizures resulting from head trauma.

**Preeclampsia:** A condition of hypertension that occurs during pregnancy.

**Progesterone:** A steroid hormone produced in the ovary. It prepares and maintains the uterus for pregnancy.

**Progressive myoclonic epilepsy:** A neurological condition characterized by myoclonic and grand mal seizures, as well as, developmental delays. It can occur during infancy

**Psychosis:** A mental disorder in which delusions and hallucinations are combined.

**Pyridoxine:** Vitamin $B_6$.

**Quadrantonopia:** Defect in the peripheral vision or a visual field defect in the right or left quadrant.

**Reduced penetrance:** The mutated gene effect is modified or reduced and does not always cause disease when present.

**Reflex epilepsies:** Epilepsies that are triggered by specific stimuli.

**Resection:** Excision of a portion or all of an organ or other structure.

**Seizure:** An abnormal clinical behavior as a result of excessive excitation of brain cells.

**Seizure focus:** Where the seizure is originating; also called the "seizure foci."

**Seizure threshold:** A person's resistance to seizures that can be inherited. Patients with a low seizure threshold have a higher propensity for seizures.

**Selective serotonin reuptake inhibitors(SSRIs):** Medications used to treat depression, anxiety or other psychiatric conditions. They slow down the ability of nerve cells to absorb serotonin.

**Simple febrile seizures:** Seizures occurring in relation to a high fever; usually brief grand mal seizure without any focal features.

**Simple partial seizure:** A partial seizure where the person remains fully conscious but experiences unusual sensations such as strange tastes or smells, feelings of fear or déjà vu, or involuntary twitching of limbs.

**Single photon emission computerized tomography(SPECT):** A type of brain scan that gives information about the function and structure of the brain.

**Spinal bifida:** A congenital defect in the spinal column. There is an absence of vertebral arches and coverings or the whole spinal cord may be protruding.

**Status epilepticus:** Seizures continuing for prolonged time, usually more than 30 minutes, without returning to baseline.

**Stroke:** Death of brain tissue that usually results from obstruction to the blood flow of the brain.

**Sturge-Weber syndrome:** A congenital disease present at birth and characterized by a facial birthmark or port-wine stain (reddish brown or pink discoloration of the face). This vascular birthmark is caused by an overabundance of capillaries, a type of blood vessel, located just beneath the surface of the affected skin. These malformed blood vessels in the brain may cause neurological abnormalities, such as, progressive mental retardation, epilepsy, and glaucoma in the eye on the affected side.

**Subdural strips:** This is a strip of electrodes that can be slid beneath the brain covering to localize the seizure onset.

**Subependymal nodule:** These are composed of calcified glia (supporting cells of the brain) and vascular elements that are found in the ventricles.

**Sudden unexpected death in epilepsy:** A sudden, unexpected death of someone with epilepsy, but who was otherwise healthy, and for whom no other cause of death can be found.

**Symptomatic epilepsy:** Epilepsy where the cause of the condition is known.

**Synapses:** Contact points where the communication between neurons is polarized.

**Syncopal episodes:** Transient loss of consciousness due to decreased blood supply to the brain.

**Syndrome:** A combination of signs and/or symptoms occurring together indicating a particular disorder.

**Temporal binding:** Local network systems in the brain that play important role in cognition and perception.

**Temporal lobe epilepsy:** Epilepsy where the seizures originate in the temporal lobe of the brain. The seizures are usually complex partial seizures.

**Temporal lobe:** The part of the brain that is involved in speech, language, memory, and the perception of smell and taste.

**Temporal lobectomy:** A procedure to remove part of the brain that is involved with speech, language, memory, and the perception of smell and taste.

**Teratogenic:** Substances or agents that can interfere with normal embryonic development.

**Testosterone:** A potent androgenic hormone produced chiefly by the testes and responsible for the development of male secondary sex characteristics.

**Tetany:** Muscle spasm that can benefit from magnesium and calcium supplements.

**Therapeutic range:** The range of drug levels within which most patients will experience significant therapeutic effect without adverse side effects. The ranges quoted should be used as a guide only because individual patients may have

differences in drug distribution or transport, which alter drug availability at the receptor.

**Todd's paresis:** Paralysis of temporary duration that occurs after a seizure.

**Tomography:** The technique of using rotating x-rays to capture an image at a particular depth in the body, bringing those structures into sharp focus while blurring structures at other depths.

**Tonic seizures:** Generalized seizures where a person's body becomes stiff and he or she may fall backward. The seizure usually lasts less than one minute and recovery is rapid.

**Toxicity:** Adverse side effects of a drug on a patient.

**Tonic seizures:** A violent muscular contraction.

**Tonic–clonic seizure:** This is a generalized seizure, also called convulsion or grand mal.

**Tracer:** A substance, usually radioactively labeled, that is injected into your body and can be followed to gain information about metabolic processes.

**Transcranial magnetic stimulation:** In this type of electromagnetic therapy, an insulated coil is placed against the head, and an electrical current generates a magnetic field into the brain.

**Transient ischemic attacks:** Ministrokes caused by brief ischemia.

**Tremor:** Involuntary trembling, usually of the hands or head, that can involve the legs, the tongue, or palate.

**Tuberous sclerosis:** A neurological condition associated with seizures, mental retardation, and skin lesions. Multiple organs such as skin, heart, brain, kidneys, and eyes can be involved.

**Tubers:** Abnormal disorganized large neuron cells in the cortex. Also seen in tuberous sclerosis.

**Vagal nerve stimulator:** A small generator implanted in a person's chest. The generator stimulates the vagus nerve that may prevent the abnormal brain activity that gives rise to a seizure.

**Vasovagal attacks:** A temporary vascular reaction associated with rapid fall in heart rate and blood pressure.

**Ventricles:** Hollow cavities in the brain filled with cerebrospinal fluid.

**Video EEG:** A test involving simultaneous EEG and video recording.

**West syndrome:** A syndrome characterized by infantile spasms, mental retardation, and a specific EEG pattern (hypsarrhythmia).

# *Index*